CADOGAN CHESS BOOKS

Chess Middlegames: Essential Knowledge

CADOGAN CHESS BOOKS

Chief Advisor: Garry Kasparov
Editor: Andrew Kinsman
Russian Series Editor: Ken Neat

Other titles in this series include:

AVERBAKH, Y.
Chess Endings: Essential Knowledge

BRONSTEIN, D.
The Modern Chess Self-Tutor

BRONSTEIN, D.
 & FÜRSTENBERG, T.
The Sorcerer's Apprentice

GELLER, Y.
The Application of Chess Theory

GUFELD, E.
An Opening Repertoire for the
 Attacking Player

KASPAROV, G.
Garry Kasparov's Chess Puzzle Book

LIVSHITZ, A.
Test Your Chess IQ Books 1-3

NEISHTADT, I.
Winning Quickly with White
Winning Quickly with Black

POLUGAYEVSKY, L.
Grandmaster Achievement
Grandmaster Performance

POLUGAYEVSKY, L.
 & DAMSKY, I.
The Art of Defence in Chess

SHEKHTMAN, E. (Compiler)
The Games of Tigran Petrosian

SHERESHEVSKY, M.
Endgame Strategy

SHERESHEVSKY, M.
 & SLUTSKY, L.
Mastering the Endgame Vols. 1 & 2

SMYSLOV, V.
Smyslov's 125 Selected Games

TAIMANOV, M.
Taimanov's Selected Games

TAL, M. & DAMSKY, I.
Attack with Mikhail Tal

For a complete catalogue of CADOGAN CHESS books (which includes the former Pergamon Chess and Maxwell Macmillan Chess list) please write to:

Cadogan Books, London House, Parkgate Road, London SW11 4NQ
Tel: (0171) 738 1961
Fax: (0171) 924 5491

Chess Middlegames: Essential Knowledge

by

Yuri Averbakh

Translated and Edited by Ken Neat

CADOGAN
chess
LONDON, NEW YORK

English Translation Copyright © 1996 Ken Neat

First published 1996 by Cadogan Books plc, London House, Parkgate Road, London SW11 4NQ.

Distributed in North America by Simon and Schuster, Paramount Publishing, 200 Old Tappan Road, Old Tappan, New Jersey 07675, USA.

British Library Cataloguing in Publication Data
A CIP catalogue record for this book is available from the British Library

ISBN 1 85744 125 7

Cover design by Brian Robins

Typeset by Ken Neat, Durham

Printed in Great Britain by BPC Wheatons Ltd, Exeter

Contents

Introduction		7
1	A Little about Strategy and Tactics	8
2	Elementary Contacts	12
3	Attack and Defence	15
4	Tying and Pinning	18
5	Combined Attack	22
6	Second Wave of the Attack	26
7	Double Attack	28
	One piece simultaneously attacks two enemy pieces	28
	Two pieces simultaneously attack one enemy piece	30
	Two pieces simultaneously attack two enemy pieces	32
8	Reciprocal Double Attack	36
9	Double Blow	38
10	Defence against a Double Blow	42
11	How a Double Blow Arises	46
12	Attack on the King	53
13	Mating Attack Mechanisms	57
14	Combinations and Sacrifices	62
15	Classification of Combinations	70
16	Winning Combinations	73
	Combinations against the king	73
	Combinations to win material	76
	Combinations to promote a pawn	77
17	Drawing Combinations	79
	Perpetual check	79
	Stalemate	80
	Blockade	81
	Perpetual pursuit	82
	Fortress	83
	Drawing balance of forces	85
18	Chess Aesthetics	87

19   Strategy of Attack   95
         Attack on the uncastled king   95
         Attack on the kingside   98
         Attack after castling on opposite sides   103
         Attack on the queenside   107

Index of Players and Analysts   111

Introduction

The middlegame is the most difficult and complicated phase of chess, but also undoubtedly the most fascinating and interesting. Many major works have been devoted to it, and in various books one can find hundreds of examples from the middlegame, but it seems to me that such a mass of material is most likely to frighten the average chess enthusiast, wishing to improve his play in this stage of the game in order to achieve certain successes, and, more important, to obtain the maximum pleasure from playing.

It was for this reason that the author had the idea of writing a small book devoted to the middlegame, and including in it only that which is most important, most essential, so that subsequently the reader would be able independently and competently to solve many problems arising during the struggle on the chess board.

Since the middlegame is the most complicated phase of chess, as with any complicated phenomenon various approaches can be made to it. Since the main aim of the game is to give mate to the enemy king, which demands a certain coordination of the forces, I consider that particular attention should be devoted to the problems of concerted piece action.

In this book I have tried to reveal to the reader the deep significance of these important concepts, and have aimed to show how the coordination of the pieces arises during play. My main conclusion, which will make it much easier to understand the basic struggle on the chess board, is that, despite the countless multitude of different situations arising in the middlegame, there are only two effective attacking procedures, leading to success – the combined attack and the double blow. A mastery of these techniques, and an ability to prepare them gradually, is extremely important.

And one more thing. Since in the middlegame the main target of attack is his majesty the king, in this book great attention has been paid to the attack on the king. Typical mating mechanisms, offensive techniques, and ways of conducting an attack are all considered.

The task of this small book is to help the reader to find his way through the boundless ocean of chess, in which, according to the Indian saying: 'a gnat may drink and an elephant may bathe.'

Yuri Averbakh
November 1995

1 A Little about Strategy and Tactics

During the course of a game a player repeatedly has to find answers to two questions – what to do, and how to do it. The answer to the first question is given by chess strategy, and to the second by tactics.

It is well known that, in warfare, strategy is assigned the leading role, and tactics a subordinate one.

But on the chess board everything is different. Although here too tactics are largely subordinate to strategy, their role is extremely important. After all, on the chess board, except when a pawn is promoted, there are no reserves, and this means there can be no addition to the existing forces, which themselves are very limited. Therefore it is not surprising that even one tactical mistake, oversight or blunder may lead to defeat. And on the contrary, a successful tactical operation may immediately decide the outcome of a game. During play, especially in complicated, unclear positions, you have to be extremely attentive. Otherwise unpleasant surprises will await you at every step.

Remember that, however successful your strategical plan, a tactical mistake can completely ruin it. Not without reason is it said that, to win

a game, forty moves or more may be required, but to lose it is sufficient to make one bad one! You yourself will no doubt have several times encountered this paradox. As grandmaster Richard Teichmann once aptly put it: 'chess is 90 per cent tactics!' Every player, from beginner to World Champion, has experienced this at first hand himself.

In order to gain an impression of the connection between strategy and tactics on the chess board, we will examine a short, but highly instructive game, played by two Moscow masters of roughly the same strength. This game, incidentally, also demonstrates certain ideas and procedures typical of the middle-game.

Bonch-Osmolovsky–Baranov
Moscow 1953

1 e4 e5
2 ♘f3 ♘f6

Instead of defending his e5 pawn, Black in turn attacks the opponent's pawn. This opening, developed by Russian masters in the 19th century, is called the Petroff Defence.

It should be known that if 3 ♘xe5 Black should first play 3...d6, and only then take the e4 pawn. The point is that on the immediate 3...♘xe4 White has the strong reply 4 ♕e2, when the knight cannot move on account of 5 ♘c6+, winning the queen.

| 3 | d4 |

White, with the advantage of the opening move, is the first to begin play in the centre, simultaneously opening lines for the development of his pieces.

3	...	exd4
4	e5	♘e4
5	♕xd4	d5
6	exd6	♘xd6
7	♗d3	♕e7+

Experience has shown that 7...♘c6 8 ♕f4 g6 is more accurate here. With the move in the game Black plans to answer 8 ♗e3 with 8...♘f5, exchanging knight for bishop. But as we will see later, this operation leads to a loss of time, and to Black delaying the development of his pieces.

| 8 | ♗e3 | ♘f5 |

It was not yet too late for Black to reject his initial plan. By playing 8...♗f5 9 ♘c3 ♘c6 10 ♕a4 ♗xd3 he would have gained an acceptable position, whereas now he encounters significant problems.

| 9 | ♗xf5 | ♗xf5 |
| 10 | ♘c3! | |

It transpires that taking the pawn is extremely dangerous: on 10...♗xc2 there follows 11 ♖c1 ♘c6 (11...♗f5 12 ♘d5) 12 ♕f4. It is true that here Black has 12...♘b4!, but

White calmly replies 13 0-0!, and if 13...♘d3 14 ♕c4 ♘xc1 15 ♖xc1, when the bishop cannot move on account of 16 ♘d5.

Therefore with his next move Black switches his queen to the queenside, to where, to all appearances, the opponent's king is intending to take shelter.

| 10 | ... | ♕b4 |
| 11 | ♕e5+ | |

Of course, there is no point in White exchanging queens. His lead in development is best exploited in an attack.

| 11 | ... | ♗e6 |
| 12 | 0-0-0 | ♘c6 |

In the hope of mounting an attack along the c-file, Black tries to buy his opponent off with a pawn.

13	♕xc7	♖c8
14	♕f4	♕a5
15	♕g5!	

By offering the exchange (now that he is a pawn up), White

switches his queen to an active position with gain of tempo.

15 ...   ♛a6
16 ♖he1

A picturesque position. White's pieces are fully mobilised and are ready for positive action, while Black has not yet resolved the question of safeguarding his king. Therefore he decides on a desperate counterattack.

16 ...   ♞b4
17 ♞d4   ♖xc3

Naïvely assuming that this exchange sacrifice will lead to a draw. For example: 18 bxc3 ♞xa2+ 19 ♔d2 ♞xc3 20 ♔xc3 ♝b4+! 21 ♔xb4 ♛c4+ 22 ♔a3 ♛a2+ with perpetual check. But White had seen beforehand that after the capture on c3 the opponent's back rank would be weakened, which allows him to strike a decisive tactical blow.

18 ♛d8+!!

Truly a bolt from the blue!

18 ...   ♔xd8

19 ♞xe6+

Against such a check, called a double check, there is only one defence – the king has to flee, but where to? If 19...♔c8 20 ♖d8 mate, while 19...♔e8 is met by 20 ♞xg7+ ♝xg7 21 ♝g5+ ♔f8 22 ♖d8 mate. That only leaves e7, but there too the king does not find safety.

19 ...   ♔e7
20 ♝g5+!

It is important not to let the king escape to f6.

20 ...   f6
21 ♞d8+

Here Black admitted defeat: there is no defence against mate in two moves.

In this game we see a clash of two ideas, of two strategical plans. Relying on his lead in development, White concentrated his pieces in the centre, preparing an attack on the enemy king that had not managed to castle. Black, after sacrificing a pawn, was hoping for a counterattack on the queenside, where the white king had castled. But everything was decided by tactics – by sacrificing his queen, White was able to refute Black's plan and to conclude the game brilliantly.

Note that in the final mating attack all the white pieces took part (with the exception, of course, of the king). And the actions of his pieces were excellently coordinated – in the final position the rook at d1 takes away the black king's squares on the d-file and defends the knight at d8. The knight, in turn, deprives the king of the f7 square, the bishop has deprived it of the f6 square, and the rook at e1 lands the fatal blow. The bishop at f8 and pawn at f6 not only fail to help, but actually hinder their king, by depriving it of the vital squares f8 and f6. And the king's rook, like the remaining black pieces and pawns, performs the cheerless role of spectator to the execution of its own monarch.

This game demonstrates the importance of assigning roles on the chess board. And in the following chapter we will begin by trying to understand how the pieces and pawns coordinate one with another.

2   Elementary Contacts

The aim in a game of chess is to checkmate the opponent's king. But none of the pieces is able to achieve this on its own. As we know, to do this even the all-powerful queen needs help.

For success in operations carried out on the chess board, the harmonious, coordinated action of the pieces is required. It is extremely important to understand how this arises. We will try to disclose what lies behind these exceptionally important concepts.

Let us consider the initial arrangement of the pieces.

The two sides are both lined up in two ranks facing each other. Between them is a large neutral zone. All is calm and quiet – no one is threatening anyone else, and indeed no one is able to do so.

However, already in the initial disposition in each camp one can discern a number of contacts and links between the pieces and pawns, and that means, their coordination.

The pawns cover the pieces standing behind them from the attacks of the enemy pieces, and the pieces, in turn, defend (support) these pawns, each at least once, while simultaneously defending one another. However, the initial placing of the pieces also has a very significant defect – apart from the knights, none of the pieces is able to move, to say nothing of attacking the opponent's pieces: they are prevented from doing so by their own pieces and pawns, which restrict one another's freedom of action.

Thus in the initial position we discern three types of contacts between the pieces (and also between the pieces and pawns) of each side – three forms of elementary coordination.

1. Support – a piece (or pawn) supports (defends) another piece (or pawn).

2. Covering – a piece (or pawn) covers another piece (or pawn) against attack.

3. Restriction – a piece (or pawn) restricts either the movement, or the scope of another piece (or pawn).

Whereas the first two contacts may be considered useful, although not always necessary (after all, in the initial position there are as yet no threats at all), the third contact demonstrates an adverse, lack of coordination in the actions of the pieces, when they not only do not help, but essentially hinder one another.

Now let us see how the situation on the board changes after some initial opening moves. Let us play **1 e4**. White immediately takes control of the squares d5 and f5 in the opponent's territory, and at the same time certain restrictions are straight away removed – his queen, bishop and even his king gain the opportunity to move forward. But the e4 pawn has immediately broken away from its camp and, lacking support by the pieces, is undefended. And here we note the arising of a fourth contact – the **threat of an attack** on it by a black knight from f6.

After the reply **1...e5** Black takes control of the d4 and f4 squares in the opponent's territory. In addition, the white pawn is blocked. It is halted, restricted in its movements.

But the e5 pawn that has broken away from base is now itself threatened by an attack. And, by **2 ♘f3**, White carries out this threat, attacking the black pawn and creating the fifth contact – **attack**. Note that from f3 the knight also creates the threat of attacking the f7 pawn.

We come to the important conclusion that between the pieces of the opposing sides there exist three types of contacts, three types of interaction. Firstly, restriction (as mentioned earlier), secondly, the threat of an attack, and thirdly, the attack itself. Incidentally, it is useful to mention that an attack – by one piece on another – does not arise suddenly, but gradually: first there must be a threat.

By replying **2...♘c6**, Black defends the e5 pawn, controls the d4 square, and creates the threat of an attack on c2.

If we wish to, we can (relying on elementary contacts), describe any situation that arises on the chess board. Subsequently we will try to do this. But here our task is to show how, in the course of play, between the pieces of the two sides certain contacts and links arise. Figuratively speaking, as the forces of the two sides take up their fighting positions, between the warring camps there as though extend invisible lines of force. Imperceptible to the naked eye, like very fine wires, they enmesh the field of battle.

These lines of force – we call them elementary contacts and links, arise both between the pieces, and between pieces and certain squares. To repeat, these elementary links are support, covering, restriction, the threat of an attack, and the attack itself.

Strictly speaking, in the endgame another contact arises – the sixth and a very distinctive one – **the link between a passed pawn and its promotion square**. Like a magnet, the pawn is drawn towards this square, and the closer it is to it, the stronger the threat of it being promoted to a queen. This threat is no less strong that an attack on this square.

However, the promotion of a pawn is not typical of the middlegame, and here we will touch on this theme only briefly.

In conclusion it should be mentioned that all other, more complicated types of tactical interaction are formed out of these six elementary contacts that we have discovered.

3   Attack and Defence

In the course of a game the warring sides endeavour to inflict material losses on each other, and with this aim they make attacks with their pieces and pawns on the pieces and pawns of the opponent.

Let us look again at the initial position.

It is not difficult to establish that from g1 the white knight can neither attack, nor threaten to attack any of the enemy pieces. But from f3 it is threatening an attack, and from g5 or e5 it is already attacking the f7 pawn. Beginning an attack on the f7 pawn from g1, the knight moves as though by steps. Strictly speaking, even from g1 the knight is threatening to attack the f7 pawn, only for this it requires not one move, as from f3, but two. Therefore it can be said that from g1 the

knight creates a threat of the second order. Depending on the number of moves that are needed to accomplish an attack, these threats can be of various orders (stronger or weaker).

We thus come to the conclusion that, before making an attack, a piece moves as though by steps, gradually intensifying the threat. Attacks and threats (moreover, as we have established, threats can be of various orders) constitute elementary means of attack. And there is another extremely important conclusion. Whereas attacks and threats of the first order are easily discernible, threats of the second, third and subsequent orders are often concealed from the experienced eye and are not easy to spot.

Thus, an attack has been made on a piece. But how effective is it? It is effective only if the opponent disregards this threat or does not notice it. But if he sees the threat, he will try to avoid material loss, and theoretically he will have five possible ways of defending. Let us examine them in turn with the aid of a schematic position (*see diagram next page*).

Let us suppose that White has just played 1 ♖fd1, attacking the unprotected bishop at d6.

1. Withdrawal. The attacked piece moves out of the firing line. This method of defence can be either passive or active in nature. If the piece simply moves, leaving the attacked square, this will be a passive defence – here, for example, **1...♗f8**.

But if, in moving, it in turn attacks an opponent's piece, such a defence will be active. Here such an opportunity is provided by the move **1...♗f4**.

2. Support. The attacked piece remains in place, but, in order to defend it, another piece is brought up to its defence. This method allows an exchange, therefore support is normally possible only when the attacking piece is of equal or superior strength and importance to the attacked piece: otherwise the exchange will lead to material loss for the defending side. In our example the attacked bishop can be supported, for instance, by **1...♖ad8**.

3. Covering. If the attacking piece is of long-range action, then another piece can be moved into the line of attack, drawing the fire on itself. This method also allows an exchange, therefore the covering piece should normally be equal to or weaker than the attacking piece. In addition, it should be supported either by the attacked piece itself, or by some other piece. Here the attack on the bishop can be covered by **1...♘d5**.

4. Answering attack (counterattack). In this case the attack is simply disregarded, the attacked piece is left undefended, and in reply an attack is made on a stronger or at least equal piece of the opponent. In our position this might be done by **1...h6**.

5. Capture. If the attacking piece is on a square that in turn is attacked by one of the opponent's pieces, it may be captured. Here Black has the possibility of **1...♗xd1**.

These are the main methods of attack and defence. In the event of the attacked piece withdrawing (1...♗f8), or the attacking piece being captured (1...♗xd1), the situated is relieved. But in the other three cases the situation becomes more aggravated and complicated: into the conflict are drawn not just two, but a minimum of three (in the case of support or covering) or even four pieces (in the event of a counterattack).

As we have seen, the defensive

possibilities are very diverse. But their employment is often determined by the type of attacking and defending pieces. Thus, for example, if a piece is attacked by a pawn, it normally has to save itself by running away, against an attack by a knight it is impossible to defend by covering, while if the king is attacked, in this case neither support nor counterattack are possible. In short, the choice of defensive methods depends on the concrete situation.

4   Tying and Pinning

Let us suppose that some piece has attacked an equivalent or weaker piece of the opponent, and that another piece has come to its aid, by defending it. It would seem that the balance has been restored. Ah, no! Compared with the initial situation, it has significantly changed: between these three pieces a certain tension has arisen – invisible attacking and defensive lines of force are now in place.

In this case it may prove that the third, supporting piece significantly loses in strength: its mobility and ability to attack will be restricted.

It turns out that by **tying** it is possible to neutralise a significant material advantage. Let us consider, for example, the conclusion to a study by **V.Chekhover** (1949).

In this amusing position Black cannot win, even if it his turn to move. If he plays **1...♘d6**, then after **2 ♔g7**, in order not to lose a piece, the knight has to go back to f7, while if **1...♗c2**, then **2 ♔g7 ♗b3 3 ♔h7!** and the knights, which are tied to each other, are crippled.

As we see, here the king on its own successfully opposes three enemy minor pieces. And this occurs thanks to tying.

If a piece is attacked by a long-range piece, it can be defended by covering – a second piece as though takes the fire upon itself, covering the line of action of the attacking piece. In doing so it itself turns out to be **pinned**: if it moves, this will lead to the loss of the attacked piece.

In other words, after covering, the attack on the attacked piece disappears, but the threat of an attack still remains. And the pinned piece loses both in mobility and in activity.

Such a situation, in which, as in tying, a minimum of three pieces take part, is called a **pin**. By means of a pin a big material advantage can also be neutralised.

(*see diagram next page*)

Here Black is a rook up, but he cannot win.

His knight is pinned, and (since under normal circumstances king and rook cannot win against king and bishop) his king and rook are forced to defend it – they are tied to it. White achieves a draw by moving his bishop between g3 and h2.

The following position is perhaps even more amazing.

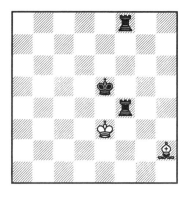

Black has an enormous material advantage – two rooks against a bishop, but here too his attempts to win come to nothing.

These two examples demonstrate that a pin is especially important, if the pinned piece is covering the king: in this case it completely loses its strength! This feature of a pin is sometimes forgotten even by masters. Here is a typical example.

Makogonov–Chekhover
Tbilisi 1937

White had aimed for this position from a long way off. He was not afraid of **1...♖f8**, since he assumed that by **2 ♖d8** he in turn would pin the enemy rook. But the experienced master had not taken account of the fact that his pinned queen had lost his strength and that **2...♕h4+!** was possible, after which he was immediately obliged to capitulate.

The defects of pinned pieces, covering their king, are also strikingly demonstrated by the following ancient study.

C.Gilbert, 1877
White to play and mate in two

By playing **1 ♕f1!** White does not appear to threaten anything: all the approaches to the enemy king are securely defended. But the problem is that it is Black to play, and a move by any of his pieces disrupts the defence. Thus on a knight move there follows **2 ♕f6 mate**, on a rook move **2 ♕f4 mate**, and finally, if **1...♔xe6+ 2 ♕f5 mate**. This final position merits a diagram.

The queen at f5 is under attack by four black pieces – king, queen, rook and pawn, but not one of them can take it. The king, because the queen is supported by its own king, and the remaining three pieces because they are pinned, the black king being behind them. It thus transpires that the four-fold defence of the f5 square is in fact illusory.

If it is the queen or some other piece, apart from the king, of course, that is behind the pinned piece, then in certain circumstances such a pin can be disregarded.

A classic example of such an 'illusory' pin is provided by the ancient miniature game **Legall de Kermeur-St Brie**, played in Paris in 1750.

1 e4 e5 2 ♗c4 d6 3 ♘f3 ♗g4 4 ♘c3 g6

The knight at f3 is pinned, but it unexpectedly releases itself:

5 ♘xe5! ♗xd1

Black's greed is his undoing. Of course, he should have replied

5...dxe5, losing only a pawn. But now he is mated in two moves.

6 ♗xf7+ ♔e7 7 ♘d5 mate.

This spectacular finish became known as 'Legall's mate'.

And here is another example of unpinning that has become a classic.

(*see diagram next column*)

Not seeing how he could save his pinned bishop, Black resigned. But he could have not only saved the game, but even won with the spectacular move **1...♗g1!** Attacking the queen with his rook, Black simultaneously threatens mate at h2. And here it is White who would have had to resign!

It can be said that a pin is 'illusory', if the pinned piece is able to release itself, by creating some strong threat, such as the threat of mate, the threat to win a stronger piece, and so on.

von Popiel–Marco
Monte Carlo 1902

5   Combined Attack

As we have already stated, a simple attack on an enemy piece rarely proves effective. For this to happen it has to be incapable of being defended or covered by its own pieces, and of moving out of the attack.

Quite a different matter is a combined attack, normally carried out by several pieces or pawns, when one of them attacks the opponent's piece, and the others prevent it from moving or being defended. In such situations it often happens that the withdrawal squares of the piece are cut off by its own pieces or pawns.

Nimzowitsch–Alekhine
Bled 1931

Here all White's hopes rest on his attack on the rook at a8, but Black found a refutation of his plan: **1... ♘d5+ 2 ♗d2 ♕b6 3 ♕xa8+ ♔d7**, and the white queen is trapped. After **4 0-0-0 ♘c7 5 ♗a5 ♘xa8 6 ♗xb6 ♘xb6** Black won.

Averbakh–Boudi-Bueno
Polanica Zdroj 1975

In this position White played **1 f4! ♕xe4 2 ♖e1**, and it transpired that the black queen was trapped. After **2...e6 3 ♘xf6** Black resigned.

In this position, the conclusion to a study by **L.Kubbel** (1940), Black does not look to be in any particular danger.

But there follows **1 ♕a8! ♔b2 2 ♘d5**, and White manages to deprive the queen of all eight free squares. Note the negative role played here by the black pawns, which significantly restrict the freedom of their own queen.

Andersson–E.Torre
Biel 1977

White played **1 ♖b3**, reckoning on regaining his pawn, but after **1...b4! 2 ♖xb4 b5 3 h5 ♗d6 4 ♖b3 b4** his rook was trapped. By continuing **5...♖e8** followed by taking his king to c4, Black won.

In the following position White's first move **1 ♕c1** looks incomprehensible, and Black decided to win the opponent's central pawns by **1...♘xd4+ 2 ♔d3 ♕xe5**. But White had calculated accurately: **3 ♕c8+ ♔g7 4 ♕h8+! ♔xh8 5 ♘xf7+ ♔g7**

6 ♘xe5, and the black knight had no retreat.

Matulovic–Cvetkovic
Varna 1965

In one of the variations of the Ruy Lopez after **1 e4 e5 2 ♘f3 ♘c6 3 ♗b5 a6 4 ♗a4 d6 5 d4 b5 6 ♗b3 ♘xd4 7 ♘xd4 exd4** the following position is reached.

Here **8 ♕xd4** would be a mistake on account of **8...c5 9 ♕d5 ♗e6 10**

♕c6+ ♗d7 11 ♕d5 c4, when the white bishop is trapped.

In the examples considered the targets of the combined attack were the queen, rook, knight and bishop. But a king can also be subjected to a combined attack. We will give several typical instances of an attack on the king, where the decisive blow is landed by various pieces.

Of course, the strongest piece in an attack on the king is the queen.

Soultanbiev–Colle
Liège 1926

Tarjan–Karpov
Skopje 1976

White has created the threat of mate in two moves, but it is Black to play, and he wins by **1...♖e3+! 2 fxe3 ♕g3 mate**.

By pinning the rook at f3 (*see next diagram*), Black assumed that he had defended against all the threats. But after **1 ♖g2!** it transpired that the rook could not be taken on account of 2 ♕xf8 mate, and meanwhile 2 ♕xh7+ ♔xh7 3 ♖h3 mate was threatened.

N.N.–Pillsbury
Blindfold Exhibition 1899

In this position Black gives mate with a lone bishop, only first he has to restrict the enemy king: **1...♕f1+ 2 ♔g1**, and now **2...♕f3+! 3 ♗xf3 ♗xf3 mate**.

As we see, in the final mating position the task of restricting the king is fulfilled by pieces of the same colour. Picturesquely speaking, they as though go over to the opponent's side, by hindering their own king.

A similar situation arises when mate is given by a lone knight. A classic example is the so-called 'smothered mate', which has been known since the late 15th century, at the dawn of modern chess.

1 ♕e6+ ♔h8 2 ♘f7+ ♔g8 3 ♘h6+ ♔h8 4 ♕g8+! ♖xg8 5 ♘f7 **mate**.

Mate by a pawn occurs most often in the endgame, but here we give one of the rare examples of a spectacular mate of this type in the middlegame.

Georgadze–Kuindzhi
Tbilisi 1973

In this unusual position both kings are in danger, and in fact White is threatening mate in one move. But it is Black to play, and in three moves he is the first to give mate: **1...♕f2+! 2 ♕xf2 ♖h5+! 3 ♗xh5 g5 mate**.

I hope that you will have understood that in the event of a combined attack on enemy pieces, including the king, it is extremely important not only to coordinate the actions of your own pieces, but also to be able to exploit the restricting role played by the opponent's pieces.

6 Second Wave of the Attack

Let us suppose that the first attack has been parried: an adequate defence against it has been found. The attacked piece has been supported or covered against attack by another piece, or, finally, a counterattack has been employed.

However, the battle is not yet over. If the attacker has reserves – pieces occupying active positions – then a second wave of the attack is quite possible – a new attack.

If the attacked piece has been supported, then here there are theoretically two possible attacking options:

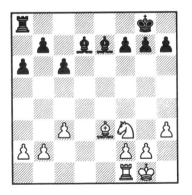

1. A second attack on the defended piece. Since it is carried out by a new piece, this will already be a double attack, in which two pieces attack one. In such situations the attacked piece most often has to safe itself by running away.

Thus in the above schematic position White may attack the black bishop at d7 with **1 ℤd1**. If Black defends it by **1...ℤd8**, then White can attack the bishop a second time with **2 ♘e5**, forcing it to move.

2. An attack on the supporting piece. This attack is even more dangerous than the previous one. After all, it is not so simple for the supporting piece simply to leave its post, without abandoning its 'ward' to its fate. Here too there is a double attack: two pieces attack two enemy pieces. Moreover, if the defending piece is not in turn supported by some other piece or pawn, this entire defensive construction may collapse like a house of cards in the face of the second attack.

In our schematic position after **1 ℤd1 ℤd8** this could be carried out by **2 ♗b6**.

If the defence is carried out by covering, then again there are theoretically two attacking options.

1. A second attack on the covered piece, only this time from a different, undefended side.

In the following schematic position Black might answer **1 ♗b3**, attacking his rook, with the covering move **1...♘d5**. Then **2 ♘d4** would be a new attack on the covered piece.

2. A new attack on the covering piece. This will be an attack of two pieces on one, which here could be made after **1 ♗b3 ♘d5** by **2 ♖ad1**.

If the defence is carried out by a counterattack, a second attack on the attacked piece is now pointless. The most effective form of attack here will be one where, in moving out of the line of fire, the attacked piece itself strikes a blow at some enemy piece. In this case two of the opponent's pieces will now be under attack.

A practical example is provided by the following position.

Black attacks the white knight with **1...c6**. If White ignores this and makes the counter-attacking move **2 ♖f3?**, then Black replies **2...♘e5**, not only defending his f7 pawn, but also attacking the rook at

f3, so that two white pieces are now threatened. Since **3 ♘f6+ ♚g7** does not help White, he is bound to lose material.

Maciewski–Averbakh
Polanica Zdroj 1976

Thus, in the second wave of the attack the defending pieces drawn into the skirmish may themselves become its target, and in many cases a double attack situation arises on the board.

Every chess enthusiast is familiar with the 'fork' – a dangerous attacking procedure, when two pieces simultaneously come under attack by a piece or pawn. As you have probably already realised, the 'fork' is merely a particular instance of a double attack. But a double attack is much more dangerous and effective than a simple one, and in tactical operations on the chess board it plays an extremely important role.

7   Double Attack

The fact that the double attack is a highly effective attacking method, was clear to our ancestors back at the dawn of modern chess. Thus, for example, in one of the first chess books – that of the Portuguese author Damiano (Rome 1512), in a chapter devoted to subtleties of play, out of a couple of dozen examples no less than half comprise various forms of double attack.

And this is what was written, for example, in the ancient book of the first Russian master Alexander Petroff (St Petersburg 1824):

'It is needful to endeavour to make such moves that would have a double aim', and 'One must also endeavour to carry out double attacks'.

Let us consider the most commonly occurring instance of a double attack.

One piece simultaneously attacks two enemy pieces

This is our familiar 'fork'. Usually it is assumed that a 'fork' is made either by a knight, or by a pawn, but in fact such an attack can be made by any piece, including his majesty the king.

But let us begin with the queen; the double attack comes into its arsenal, of course.

Uhlmann–Averbakh
Dresden 1956

By **1...♘f3** Black forces his opponent to give up rook for knight, and then by a double attack he also wins the second rook.

If, for example, White replies 2 ♖c8+ ♔g7 3 ♖xf3, there follows 3...♕xf3+ 4 ♔h2 ♕g3+ 5 ♔h1 ♕h3+ 6 ♔g1 ♕xg4+ and 7...♕xc8.

White in fact played **2 ♕d8+ ♔g7 3 ♖xf3 ♕xf3+ 4 ♔h2 ♕f4+ 5 ♔g2 ♕xg4+**, and here he resigned.

On 5...♕xg4+ there could have followed 6 ♔f2 ♕f4+ 7 ♔e2 ♕xc1 8 ♕xd5 ♕c2+ 9 ♔e3 ♕c6 10 ♕e5+ ♕f6 etc.

As regards the character of the attack, in no way different from the 'fork' is the double attack on some enemy pieces by a bishop or rook. The only difference is that the bishop attacks along diagonals, and the rook along ranks and files.

Krogius–Gauffin
Helsinki 1937

By **1 &e7** White temporarily sacrifices a piece, in order after **1...&xe7 2 &xe5** to carry out a double attack on queen and bishop and to win a pawn.

Smyslov–Zita
Prague 1946

Here Black is threatening the discovered check 1...&c2+, and 1 &c5 can be met by 1...&xg2+ 2 &xg2 &d2+ and 3...&xc1. But White, exploiting in turn the possibility of a double attack, quickly decides the game in his favour.

1 &xc4 &d2 2 &c2+! &xc2 3 &xc2 &xc2 4 &e4+ and **5 &xc2**.

Averbakh–Taimanov
Zurich 1953

In this curious position White is threatening to capture on h5 followed by the 'fork' 2 &xg7+.

The knight cannot retreat to f6 on account of 2 &f4, winning the queen, and 1...g6 allows 2 &d4. It follows that here Black has no way of defending against the double attack.

He played **1...&c8**, and after **2 &xh5+ &xh5 3 &xg7+ &d7 4 &xh5** he was two pawns down, and, of course, went on to lose.

Ahues–Kurpun
Germany 1935

By the exchange sacrifice **1 ♖xd6!** White succeeds in carrying out a pawn fork. After 1...♖xd6 or 1...♕xd6 there follows 2 e5, since 2...♕xe5 allows the decisive 3 ♗f4.

After **F.Sackmann**, 1910

Here Black has an enormous material advantage, but after **1 ♔d5**, with a double attack on the rooks, it transpires that he is unable to realise his advantage. The promotion of one of the pawns is threatened, and 1...♖cd6+ is met by 2 ♔c5, with the threat of 3 c8=♕+, while if 1...♖ed6+ 2 ♔e5, with the threat of 3 e8=♕+. Black has nothing better than to give perpetual check.

Two pieces simultaneously attack one enemy piece

The most effective example of such an attack is the double check, when both pieces simultaneously attack the king, and there is nothing else for it to do but move. The following famous old study vividly demonstrates the power of the double check.

A.White, 1919

Forced to run from the attacks of the white pieces, the black king ends up in the corner of the board, where it is mated.

1 ♖f2+ ♔e3 2 ♖f3+ ♔e4 3 ♖e3+ ♔d4 4 ♖e4+ ♔d5 5 ♖d4+ ♔c5 6

⊞d5+ ♚c6 **7** ⊞c5+ ♚b6 **8** ⊞c6+ ♚b7 **9** ⊞b6+ ♚a7 **10** ⊞b7+ ♚a8 **11** ⊞a7+ ♚b8 **12** ⊞a8 **mate**.

A mating attack, involving the use of the double check, was carried out by White in the following example.

Fridstein–Aronin
Moscow 1949

Things don't seem to be so bad for Black: he is threatening both 1...♕xe3, and 1...♞xg4. But now came the unexpected double check **1 ♗h5+! ♚h7**.

It transpires that the rook is immune: if 1...♚xf5 2 ♗g6 mate.

2 ♗g6+ ♚g8 (2...♚g7 3 ♗d4) **3 ⊞xf6! ♕xe3 4 ♗f7+! ♚f8** (4...♚h7 would have been answered by 5 ♗g8+ and 6 ⊞xh6 mate) **5 ♗e6+ ♚e7 6 ⊞f7+**, and White gives mate in two moves: 6...♚e8 7 ⊞g8+ ♗f8 8 ⊞gxf8 mate.

Attacks in the opening on f2 or f7 often involve a double attack. Here is an instructive example, which has occurred many times even in master games.

1 e4 e5 2 ♞f3 d6 3 d4 ♞d7 4 ♗c4 ♗e7?

It is hard to believe that this natural move is a fatal mistake. Fearing the advance of the knight to g5, Black defends this square with his bishop, but disregards the d5 square which is no less important. The correct reply was 4...c6.

5 dxe5 dxe5? 6 ♕d5!

Only six moves have occurred, and the attack on f7 is already irresistible. After 6...♘h6 7 ♗xh6 Black is left a piece down.

Of course, instead of 5...dxe5 it would have been much better to play 5...♘xe5, but even in this case 6 ♘xe5 dxe5 7 ♕h5 is possible, with a double attack by the queen on e5 and f7. Black has only one move – 7...g6, and after 8 ♕xe5 White wins a pawn.

An attack by two pieces is especially dangerous, if the attacked piece is pinned. We know that a pinned piece loses significantly in mobility and strength, especially if it is covering the king, a fact that should never be forgotten.

Tischler–Yurev
Leningrad 1927

In reply to **1...dxc4** White decided to treat himself to a knight and played **2 ♗xe4**, after which Black attacked the white bishop with the spectacular move **2...♕f5!**

The game continued **3 ♖e1 ♖ae8 4 ♘c3 ♖xe4! 5 ♘xe4 ♖e8**, and Black won.

Two pieces simultaneously attack two enemy pieces

Isakov–Nikitin
Correspondence 1947

Black's position looks critical: he is threatened with the capture on d7 followed by mate with the rook at b8. But by exploiting a discovered check, he not only neutralises the threat, but also tips the scales in his favour.

1...♕d3+!!

For an instant Black gives up his queen, but in so doing he lures the opponent's king into a discovered check. On 2 ♔xd3 there follows 2...♗xc6+ with a simultaneous attack on king and queen, and then 3...♗xa4. If instead the white king moves to e1, Black replies

2...♛xb1, and there is no longer a threat of mate.

Furman–Smyslov
Moscow 1949

Here White found the deadly move **1 ♛b2!** By placing his queen in ambush, he creates the threat of 2 ♘xg6+ hxg6 3 ♖h3 mate, or 2...♛xg6 3 ♖g3+ and mate next. How can this be parried? If, for example, 1...h6, then 2 ♖c7!, and if 2...♛xb2 3 ♘xg6 mate.

After the comparatively best **1...♘c4 2 ♘xg6+ ♛xg6 3 ♖xc4+ ♛g7 4 ♛xg7+ ♚xg7 5 ♖c7+** White gained a won ending.

Discovered check is the driving mechanism of the complicated tactical operation known as the 'windmill', a classic example of which is provided by the following game (*see diagram next column*).

By **1 ♗f6!!** White gave up his queen, but after **1...♛xh5 2 ♖xg7+** the 'windmill' went into operation: **2...♚h8 3 ♖xf7+ ♚g8 4 ♖g7+ ♚h8**

5 ♖xb7+ ♚g8 6 ♖g7+ ♚h8 7 ♖g5+, and White gained a winning material advantage.

K.Torre–Em.Lasker
Moscow 1925

The following study demonstrates a somewhat different construction of the 'windmill', which might well be called a 'meat-grinder'.

W.Mees, 1973

White has only three pieces, whereas Black has four times more, but the 'meat-grinder' begins to operate:

1 &xe2+ &e1 2 &b5+ ⁤e5 3 Xxe5+ &e2 4 Xxe2+ &f1 5 Xe4+ ⁤d3+ 6 &xd3+ Xe2 7 &xe2+ &e1 8 &g4+ &f1 9 &d2

After disposing of a fair number of the enemy pieces with a series of discovered checks, White begins playing for mate. Although the conclusion to the study does not relate to our theme, we nevertheless give it:

9...Xxg4 10 Xxg4 h1=⁤ 11 Xc4 with inevitable mate.

We conclude our demonstration of the strength of the discovered check with the spectacular finish to the following study.

J.Hoch, 1973

Black has queen for rook, and it appears that White is simply obliged to take the opponent's queen, and be satisfied with a draw. But he rejects the capture and makes the para-doxical move **1 &d7!!**

It transpires that White intends, exploiting the threat of a discovered check, to win the queen for nothing. Black has nothing better than to again place his queen en prise to the bishop – **1...⁤h3!**, but then **2 Xf5+ &b4 3 Xf4+** is possible, when a discovered check again leads to the win of the enemy queen. An amusing position, wouldn't you agree?

Note that here the black knight played a negative role, in helping White to trap the queen. Had it not been there, Black would have had the saving reply **1...⁤h7!**

As we have already mentioned, a double attack can also arise if, in reply to an attack, in moving out of the line of fire the attacked piece in turn attacks some opposing piece.

The following game shows that even the strongest players in the world can sometimes overlook the possibility of such an attack.

Thomas–Euwe
Nottingham 1936

By playing here 1...♗c5+ 2 ♔h1 ♘e6, Black would have achieved a perfectly acceptable position.

But he replied **1...♘e6**, assuming that the bishop at d6 could not be taken on account of 2 ♖xd6 ♖xd6 3 ♕xd6 ♖d8. However, in his preliminary calculations he overlooked the fact that White can reply 4 ♘d7!, and after 4...♕xd6 5 ♖xd6 the move 5...♘f8 is refuted by 6 ♘f6+. 5...♔h8 also does not help, if only because of 6 ♘e5.

The most interesting thing is that White believed Black, that the piece could not be taken, and replied **2 g3**.

(*see diagram next column*)

White played **1 dxc6**, not fearing possible double attacks, since he had accurately calculated the possible continuations. The game continued **1...♗xc2**.

Black has attacked all three of the opponent's heavy pieces, but after **2 ♖xd8+ ♖xd8** White struck an answering double blow with **3 ♗xf7+**, which after **3...♕xf7 4 ♕xc2** left him two pawns up.

Maroczy–Bogoljubow
Dresden 1936

Had Black first played 1...♖xd1+ 2 ♖xd1 and only then 2...♗xc2, White's strongest reply would have been 3 ♕a2!, and if 3...♖f8 (3...♖xa2 4 ♖d8 mate) 4 ♗xf7+ ♕xf7 (4...♖xf7 5 ♖d8 mate) 5 ♕xc2.

8 Reciprocal Double Attack

Already in the preceding example we saw that the situation on the board becomes sharper, when there is a reciprocal double attack. Here is another example of the same type.

Simagin–Zagoryansky
Ivanovo 1944

Black's position looks difficult: White is threatening a decisive invasion with his second rook. However, he had planned an interesting defence, based on counterattack.

1...♖f7 2 ♖h8+ ♔d7!

A reciprocal double attack has arisen. All four rooks are en prise. Captures lead only to exchanges, but White finds a clever way out of the situation.

3 ♗c6+!

A paradoxical move! It turns out that none of the three pieces can take the bishop.

3...♖xc6 is met by 4 ♖xf7, 3...♔xc6 by 4 ♖c8+ and then 5 ♖xf7 and, finally, if 3...♘xc6 White has the decisive 4 ♖xf7+. Black is obliged to move his king.

3...♔e6 4 ♖h6+ ♖f6 5 ♗d7+!

The decisive move, based on the same double attack. White wins the exchange.

The reciprocal double attack demands attentiveness, tactical vision and precise calculation, otherwise it can lead instantly to loss of material.

Here are two instructive examples from master practice.

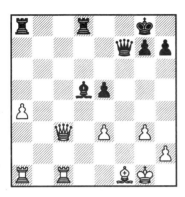

Alatortsev–Konstantinopolsky
Tbilisi 1937

Chekhover–Kan
Leningrad 1933

In this sharp position White is a pawn up, but his kingside is weakened and 1...♕f3 is threatened. All the threats could have been parried by 1 ♖c2!, in order to answer 1...♕f3 with 2 ♗g2. But White wanted immediately to solve all his problems, by exchanging the dangerous bishop, and here is what this led to:

1 ♗c4 ♗xc4 2 ♕xc4 ♖d1+!

Exploiting the fact the white rook is tied to the queen, Black creates a reciprocal double attack, which he turns to his advantage. After 3 ♔g2 ♕xc4 4 ♖xc4 ♖xa1 he is a rook up.

In the following position Black was tempted by the a2 pawn, relying on the possibility of a counter double attack.

After **1...♕xa2** and the reply **2 ♖a1** he played **2...♖xd6.**

Note that 2...♕c2 would have been bad on account of 3 ♗e4, when the queen no longer has anywhere to go.

However, he had not taken into account White's subtle reply **3 ♕e5!**

Note that, in moving out of the firing line, the queen has not only maintained the double attack, but has itself also attacked the black bishop. Here Black had been relying on the new attack 3...f6, but only now did he notice the counter possibility of a double attack by 4 ♕d5+! ♖xd5 5 ♗xd5+ and 6 ♖xa2 with a decisive advantage.

He had to reply **3...♕d2**, and after **4 ♕xb5** White went on to win.

9   Double Blow

'Excuse me', may ask the meticulous reader, who has attentively acquainted himself with the preceding pages of this book. 'Is not the double attack, which you have described in such detail, the same as the double blow?'

Yes, it is, but the double blow is a broader concept than the double attack. We define a double blow as being a combination of any two attacks and threats.

We will now consider various instances of such blows.

Chigorin–Janowski
Paris 1900

After **1 f5!** ♗xf5 White struck a double blow with **2 ♕c5**. He is threatening mate at f8, and simultaneously the bishop is attacked. Black resigned.

This is a typical instance of a double blow, consisting of an attack on an enemy piece and a threat of mate. After all, the threat of giving mate is even more dangerous than an attack.

A similar, although slightly different situation is depicted in the following example.

By **1 ♕f5** the white queen, supported by the bishop, attacks h7, threatening mate. Simultaneously it keeps under fire, i.e. attacks, the bishop at f6, although for the moment it is defended. But this is the problem! In order to defend against the mate, Black is obliged to advance his pawn to g6, thereby depriving the bishop of its defence. Thus here too we have a double blow, consisting of an attack on a piece and a threat of mate.

Balashov–Biyiasis
Manila 1976

Klyatskin–Yudovich
Moscow 1937

White played **1 ♕g4**, creating a threat with two pieces, queen and knight, to give mate at g7. At the same time he is threatening to give check with the knight at h6, with a double attack on the opponent's king and queen. It is not difficult to guess that we have here a double blow, consisting of two threats – a threat of mate and a threat of a double attack.

(see diagram next column)

With **1...♗e7** Black attacked the white rook. White could neither move his rook, not take the queen. He had to reply **2 ♖dh1**, after which Black implemented his second threat – a double attack: **2...♕xf4+ 3 ♖xf4 ♗g5 4 ♘e2 ♖df8**, when White resigned. Here the double threat consisted of an attack and the threat of a double attack.

An interesting case is represented in the following diagram:

Keres–Sliwa
Gothenburg 1955

By playing **1 ♕b3** White attacked the d5 pawn, simultaneously creating the latent threat after **2 ♘xf5 ♖xf5** of regaining the piece by 3

Xxe4, exploiting the pin. Thus here we have a double blow in the form of an attack and the threat of a second order attack.

It is clear that the threat of promoting a pawn to a queen may be no less strong than an attack. After all, they both have the aim of achieving material gain. Although the threat of queening a pawn occurs most often in the endgame, we give a rare example from the middlegame.

Engels–Maroczy
Dresden 1936

In this position White unexpectedly played **1 Xxb2 Wxb2 2 Wxc8+! ♘xc8 3 d7**.

We again have here a typical instance of a double blow – on the one hand White is threatening to queen his pawn by 4 d8=W+, and on the other hand, by taking the knight with 4 dxc8=W+. It is not hard to see that against these two queening threats Black has no defence.

It is time to sum up. The expanded concept of the double blow, a combination both of attacks, and of the most varied threats, enables us to make the following, extremely broad classification, encompassing all possible instances of attack.

1. Double attack.

2. Combination of simple attack and double attack.

3. Combination of simple attack and threats of various orders. Earlier we showed that, depending on how many moves were needed for the achievement of the set goal, threats can be distinguished as threats of the first, second, third order etc.

4. Combination of a double attack and threats of various orders.

5. Combination of two threats of various orders.

Such an expanded concept of the double blow enables us to understand the entire diversity of tactical operations carried out on the chess board, both simple, and the most complicated, and to disclose the mechanisms operating in them.

Note that threats can have the most diverse aims, significant and insignificant. There can be a threat to give mate, but there can also be a threat to occupy some strategically important square with a piece, and one may also try not to allow an enemy piece onto such a square. One can threaten to give stalemate, give perpetual check, or construct an impregnable fortress. And all these and similar threats can well be combined in a double blow.

I hope that you will have understood that in chess the double blow is an effective and truly universal device, both in attack and in defence.

I should once again remind you that it is necessary to distinguish between the double attack, which is merely a particular instance of the double blow, and the double blow in all its complexity. The point is that with a double attack everything is apparent, everything is clear – the attacks themselves are patently obvious. But with the double blow, especially with threats of higher orders (second, third etc.) situations arise that resemble an iceberg – the attacks are immediately evident, but the threats of higher orders are concealed, being as it were 'under water'. They have to be sought and found.

It should also be understood that double blows do not arise out of nothing. Initially threats must appear, and only then the double blow itself arises. The ability to foresee and to sense the possibility of a double blow arising, and to prepare it, is a great skill. It is an important component in the so-called combinational vision of a chess player. And it is to help the reader to develop his combinational vision that the author has set as his task.

10   Defence against a Double Blow

However strong, however dangerous a double blow, in exceptional situations a defence can be found. We will now turn to an examination of such cases.

We have here an ancient position by **I.Kling** (1849). It shows a typical double blow situation – the black king has attacked the opponent's rook, and simultaneously the queen is threatening mate. White's position looks critical, wouldn't you agree?

But there is a defence. White finds the fantastic move **1 ♖a4!!**

In moving his rook away from the attack, he at the same time covers the a1 square, defending against the mate, and in turn attacks the queen.

It is true that the rook is undefended, but it cannot be taken: on 1...♛xa4 there follows 2 ♖h3+ ♚e4 3 ♖h4+, winning the queen.

However, the most important thing is that, while attacking the queen, at the same time White has created the threat of mate by 2 ♖h3.

Black has only one defence, **1...♛c8**, but then all the same there follows **2 ♖h3+ ♛xh3 3 ♖a3+**, winning the queen with the help of the double blow.

We advise the reader to study this position carefully: it constitutes a veritable eulogy to the double blow, since the entire play of both sides is based on it.

The above example enables a simple rule to be established: a double blow may not bring the desired effect, if, in avoiding the blow, one of the attacked pieces is capable, in turn, of creating some strong threat such as mate etc. A defence against a double blow may also be provided by a counter double blow.

Therefore, when carrying out a double blow, one must look carefully so as not to run into a counter double blow, such as occurred, for example, in the following game.

Fischer–Shocron
Mar del Plata 1959

S.Kaminer, 1935

After **1 ♖c6** Black should have replied 1...♕d7, when, as shown by Fischer, White cannot play 2 ♖xc4 because of 2...♕d3, with the threat of 3...♖b1.

Instead Black played **1...♕d8**, hoping to catch his opponent in a double blow.

White went along with this – **2 ♖xe6 ♕c8**.

This was the move that Black was relying on (2...fxe6 3 ♕xe6+ and 4 ♕xe5 is hopeless for him), but White had seen a little further:

3 ♗d7!

It transpires that Black has fallen victim to his own plan: 3...♕xd7 is met by the double blow 4 ♖xg6+! Therefore he conceded defeat.

Here is another example, in which the salvation from a double blow is similarly provided by a double blow.

White has a queen for a bishop, but Black begins a dangerous mating attack:

1...♗g6+ 2 ♔a1 ♗e7!

The deadly double blow 3...♗f6+ is threatened. Events now develop swiftly:

3 ♘f3 ♗f6+ 4 ♘e5+ ♔e7

As yet it is not clear what White has achieved. We have a typical a double blow situation – the bishop at f6 is attacking the queen and simultaneously threatening mate. It is hard to imagine a worse position!

But nevertheless White wins here by the fantastic move **5 ♕h4!!**

By pinning the bishop, he parries the threatened capture on e5 and simultaneously intends to take the f4 pawn, to defend the knight. And after **5...♗xh4** the formerly pinned knight itself lands a double blow – **6 ♘xg6+** and **7 ♘xh4**.

To prevent the double blow, White exploited a pin, but it was a 'fork' that led to victory, i.e. again a double blow.

In such positions, rich in tactical possibilities, the seemingly most incredible moves are possible.

of mate with the rook at f1. If he plays 1 ♖cd1, then all the same 1...♕xd6 follows. 1 ♘c4 does not help on account of 1...♗xc4, and finally, after 1 ♖dd1 Black takes the knight at e5. It appears that White has nothing better than 1 ♘g6+ hxg6 2 ♕h3+ ♔g8 (2...♗h5 3 ♖xc7) 3 ♕e6+ with perpetual check.

But Alekhine had foreseen in advance a brilliant reply, which solves all White's problems, while keeping his extra piece. He played **1 ♕d1!!**

If 1...♗xd1, then 2 ♖xc7 is now possible.

The game concluded **1...♕a5 2 ♕xe2** (2 ♕d5 was also good) **2...♕xe5 3 ♖d5**, and Black resigned.

Alekhine–Verlinsky
Odessa 1918

Black has attacked both of the opponent's rooks with his queen, which White cannot take on account

This position could have occurred in the game **Reshevsky–Euwe** (*The Hague 1948*).

We have here a typical double blow situation – White is

threatening mate at h7 and is simultaneously attacking Black's knight with his own knight. It appears that the simplest way of defending is by **1...♘f6**, moving the knight out of the line of fire and defending h7. But this would be a decisive mistake: White has the diverting double blow **2 ♘d7!**, leading to the win of the queen.

The correct reply, parrying the attack, is 1...♗e4! If 2 ♘xe4 Black brings up his rook with gain of tempo by 2...♖fc8, while if 2 ♕xe4 he plays 2...♘f6, defending h7 and simultaneously attacking the queen.

11 How a Double Blow Arises

In the overwhelming majority of examples considered earlier, we encountered the double blow situations after they had already arisen. A double blow is especially dangerous, if it appears like a bolt from the blue. But this suddenness is a consequence of the fact that insufficient attention was paid to the threat of the double blow, and that necessary counter-measures were not taken in time.

Boleslavsky–Flohr
Budapest 1950

Black played **1...♖c8**, in order to release his knight from the defence of the c6 pawn. But in so doing he left the a6 pawn undefended, which allowed White, by carrying out a double blow, to win a pawn:

2 ♕d3!
A subtle move. First White must provoke ...g7-g6, weakening the f6 square. The immediate 2 ♕a3 does not achieve anything after 2...h6.

2...g6 3 ♕a3
Now a double blow situation has arisen. White is threatening both 4 ♘xh7, and 4 ♕xa6. And if 3...h6 he wins the exchange by 4 ♘h7!

Black replied **3...♘e6**, and after **4 ♘xe6 fxe6 5 ♕xa6** he lost a pawn.

Here is another example of the same type.

Kan–Levenfish
Tbilisi 1937

Here Black was pinning all his hopes on **1...♘d4**, clearly underestimating the following retreat by White:

2 ♕f1!

Now the bishop has to retreat, since 2...♘xf3+ 3 gxf3 leads to the loss of a piece.

2...♗e7?

As we will see later, this move is a mistake that in the end allows White to carry out a double blow. The only correct move was 2...♗f8, when after 3 ♘e5 ♕g5 4 f4 ♕e7 Black avoids loss of material. But now events develop by force.

3 ♘xd4 ♖xd4 4 ♗e2!

An excellent move; it transpires that on account of 5 ♗f3 Black cannot capture on e4.

4...♖xd1 5 ♕xd1 ♕g5 6 h4 ♕f6 7 e5 ♕g6 8 ♕d7, and White wins a piece.

Very often the emergence of a double blow is accompanied by sacrifices, demanding precise, and sometimes deep calculation.

the c-file by placing his queen at c3, and therefore the move **1...♖c8** looks perfectly natural, but it is in fact a decisive mistake, allowing White to carry out a double blow:

2 ♘xe6!

The knight cannot be taken on account of 3 ♕c3, but Black can take the rook.

2...♖xc4 3 ♘h6+!

This final blow had to be anticipated in advance. After 3...gxh6 4 ♕xh6 Black is mated, and therefore he resigned.

The sacrifices accompanying the double blow can be the most varied. For example, by means of a sacrifice the opponent's pieces can be forcibly drawn onto the necessary squares, on which immediately or within a few moves they come under a double blow.

The following examples demonstrate such situations.

Larsen–Matanovic
Zagreb 1965

White intends to seize control of

Horberg–Averbakh
Stockholm 1954

The awkward placing of White's queen, rook and bishop suggested to Black a rook sacrifice with the aim of inflicting a double blow.

1...♖c1!

For an instant, by giving up the rook, he lures the opponent's queen to c1, in order after **2 ♕xc1** to immediately win it – **2...♘e2+ 3 ♖xe2 ♕xc1+**. The remainder was simple: **4 ♔f2 ♗a6 5 ♗d3 ♕xa1 6 ♗xa6 ♕d1**, and White resigned.

Such sacrifices, leading to a double blow, are essentially standard techniques, with which every strong player should be familiar.

A classic example of sacrifices with the aim of luring the opponent's pieces into a double blow is provided by this position by **Emanuel Lasker**:

First, to lure the rook to c8, White sacrifices his rook:

1 ♖c8+ ♖xc8

If 1...♔xb7 2 ♖xd8, and the e1 square is defended.

Then, to lure the king to a7, the queen is given up:

2 ♕xa7+! ♔xa7

And now White regains with interest the sacrificed material:

3 bxc8=♘+!!

Often a double blow is preceded by a sacrifice with the aim of eliminating a defender.

Kupper–Olafsson
Zurich 1959

After **1 ♗xg7 ♔xg7** White exploited the unfortunate placing of Black's king and queen by the rook sacrifice **2 ♖xf7+!**

After 2...♖xf7 he immediately carries out the double blow by 3 ♘e6+, while if 2...♔g8 he has the decisive 3 ♖g7+! ♔h8 (3...♘xg7 4 ♕xh7 mate) 4 ♖xh7+ ♔g8 5 ♖g7+ ♔h8 6 ♖xg6.

In the following position White's pieces are dangerously impending over the opponent's king, but the opposition of the queens allows Black to carry out a double blow.

Tolush–Antoshin
Leningrad 1956

However, first he must eliminate the piece defending the white queen.
1...Ɽxd3! 2 Ɽxd3
White has to take with the rook: his queen is occupied with guarding g2.
2...Ɽe1+ 3 ♔f2 ♘e4+ 4 ♔xe1 ♛xg6, and Black won.

Rabinovich–Chekhover (variation)
Leningrad 1932

In this position it is only the f2 pawn that is protecting White against a double attack on g2. But perhaps it can be eliminated? Reasoning in this way, we find the spectacular move **1...♛g3!!**

The queen has to be taken – **2 fxg3**, whereupon there follows **2...Ɽxg2+ 3 ♔h1 Ɽdd2**, and mate cannot be prevented.

Lyubensky–Szepanek
Poland 1955

White has just landed a double blow – he has attacked the knight at d4 with his rook and is simultaneously threatening mate with the rook at a4. Of course, Black could have withdrawn his knight to c6, in order to block the rook check 2 Ɽa4+ with 2...♘a5. But after some thought, he found a better solution. Let us also try to find it.

If, for example, Black plays 1...♛c2+, then after 2 ♔e1 he

cannot land a double blow with 2...♘f3+, on account of the fact that this square is guarded by the g2 pawn. But perhaps there is a way of eliminating this pawn? It turns out that there is!

1...♗f3+!

The king cannot move to either one side or the other on account of mate in one move (2...♕c2 or 2...♘c2), while after **2 gxf3** there follows **2...♕c2+ 3 ♔e1 ♘xf3+**, when Black has achieved his aim.

The aim of a sacrifice may be, for example, the opening of lines, as a result of which a double blow can be landed.

A classic example of such a sacrifice is provided by the conclusion to the following game.

Bogoljubow–Capablanca
New York 1924

First Black sacrificed his knight – **1...♘xd4 2 cxd4**, and then he regained it with **2...♖8xc5**, when it

transpired that 3 dxc5 allows the double blow 3...♕xc5+, winning the rook at c1.

White therefore resigned.

Alster–Betak
Prague 1956

Black's position looks solid enough, wouldn't you agree? And yet this outwardly quiet situation conceals the threat of a double blow, and White can win a pawn with **1 ♗xh6!**

The point is that Black cannot take the bishop: the opening of the file after 1...gxh6 allows White to move his queen onto the same diagonal as the opponent's queen with gain of tempo – 2 ♕g3+, and after 2...♔f8 (if 2...♔h8 3 ♘xf7 mate) he can land the double blow 3 ♘g6+, winning the queen.

Such opportunities for a double blow are not always noticed even by masters. The following example is highly instructive.

Levenfish–Ryumin
Moscow 1936

White's knight is attacked, and without much thought he retreated it to g3. And yet he had the opportunity to create a double blow situation by sacrificing the knight:

1 ♘f6+! gxf6 2 exf6

In this position White has two threats. One is to give mate in two moves by 3 ♕g3+ and 4 ♕g7, and the other is to give mate in two moves by 3 ♕xf8+ ♔xf8 4 ♖d8. And against these two threats there is no defence.

The destruction of the enemy king's position, with the aim of opening lines and the subsequent landing of a double blow, decided the outcome of the following game.

Black's knight was at c6, and he has just played it to b4, attacking the a2 pawn. He only considered the reply 1 ♖c7, on which 1...♕xa2 is possible, when 2 ♘f6+ is not dangerous on account of 2...♔g6.

But the way that subsequent events developed was not at all how the commander of the black pieces had assumed.

Richter–Kasper
Benshausen 1975

1 ♘f6+! gxf6

The knight has to be taken, but this exposes the king, creating the grounds for the subsequent mating attack.

2 ♖c7+ ♔g6

Or 2...♔g8 3 ♕xh6.

3 ♕d1!

We have here a double blow situation – White attacks the rook, and at the same time threatens mate from g4.

Black therefore resigned.

Most often sacrifices are multipurpose. Thus in the following example the sacrifice is made both to open lines, and to eliminate a defender and set up a pin. But its ultimate aim is a double blow.

Stolyar–Averbakh
Leningrad 1938

There followed **1...♗xg2+!**

By this temporary sacrifice of a piece, Black opens the d-file for a subsequent rook sacrifice. At the same time, after the queen takes the bishop it is pinned, and is unable to defend the f2 square against a double blow by the knight.

2 ♕xg2 ♖xd1!

A reciprocal double blow situation has now arisen, so that White does not have time for 3 ♕xc6 on account of 3...♖xe1+.

3 ♖xd1 ♘f2+ 4 ♔g1 ♕xg2+ 5 ♔xg2 ♘xd1 6 ♖xb4 ♖xc2+ 7 ♔g1 ♖xb2, and Black was awarded a win on adjudication.

With this we conclude our discussion of sacrifices, leading to the emergence of a double blow situation, but we will continue it in later chapters where the question of mating attacks will be covered.

12   Attack on the King

In the initial position the king is covered from the front by a rank of pawns. But as soon as the central pawns advance, in order to allow the pieces to be developed, the king is deprived of its pawn protection, which is potentially dangerous. Therefore, as a rule, at the first opportunity castling is carried out and the king is taken into safety.

And, of course, there is no point in the king coming out ahead of its troops: it will immediately be assailed by the opponent's pieces.

To checkmate a king in the middle of the board, if it is not covered by its own pieces and pawns, is not a difficult task. Let us consider a single, but very typical example.

Alone, without his retinue, his majesty has gone out into the middle of the board. However, he was bold not through his own free will. White sacrificed three minor pieces to bring him out into 'clear water', and now he quickly finishes him off.

1 ♖ac1!

Undoubtedly the strongest move. White restricts the movements of the black monarch. It has available only a narrow little strip of the board, which in fact becomes the king's grave.

Mate on the move by 2 ♕d1 is threatened.

If the king tries to run back home with 1...♔d5, there follows 2 e6+ (or 2 ♕f7+ ♗e6 3 ♕f3+ ♔d4 4 ♕d1 mate) 2...♘f5 (2...♔d6 3 ♕e5 mate) 3 ♕xf5+ ♔d6 4 ♖ed1+ ♔e7 5 ♕f7 mate. And 1...♗f5 does not help on account of 2 ♕h4+ ♔d5 3 ♕c4 mate.

Even in the event of castling by the king, its safety is not always guaranteed. Even though covered by pieces and pawns, it may also come under attack. We will consider several typical patterns of mating attacks against the castled position.

Don't be surprised that on this and the following diagrams you will not see the white king. These are not positions from games, but patterns. They show only the pieces that land the final, mating blows.

Here White plays **1 f6**, attacking the g7 pawn with both queen and pawn, and threatening to give mate on this square. Black has no choice: like it or not, he has to reply **1...g6,** opening the gates and allowing the queen to go to h6. After **2 ♕h6** the fortress is transformed into a dungeon for the king from which there is no escape, and on the next move he is mated by **3 ♕g7.**

This shows the pattern of a

successful storming of the king's fortress, but not by a frontal assault, as in the preceding diagram, but from the side.

1 ♖e8+ ♖xe8 2 ♖xe8 mate

Again we see a familiar picture – the king's flight is cut off by his own pawns. If just one of the pawns had advanced, the king would have had more freedom, and there would have been no mate on the back rank.

The idea naturally suggests itself: is it not worth making an escape square beforehand, thereby for ever removing the threat of mate on the back rank? No, it is not. Any pawn advance weakens the king's fortress, and may allow the opponent's pieces to attack the king hiding behind the pawns. We will show this in some schematic examples.

Here Black has made an escape square in an unfortunate way by ...f7-f6. This allows White to carry out a mating attack with his rooks from the side.

1 ♖xg7+ ♔h8 2 ♖xh7+ ♔g8 3 ♖bg7 mate.

Two rooks are capable of generating enormous energy, especially if they have broken through onto the penultimate rank.

Here we see an example of a combined mating attack with rook and bishop:

1 ♖g7+ ♔h8 2 ♖xg6+ ♖f6 3 ♗xf6 mate

1 ♗f6+ ♔g8

The king cannot escape: 1...♔h6 is answered by 2 ♖h4 mate, but now too after 2 ♖h4 Black has no defence against 3 ♖h8 mate.

This is an example of a mating attack with bishop and knight. White forces mate in two moves:

1 ♘xg6+ ♔g8 2 ♘e7 mate.

Also possible is 1 ♘xf7+ ♔g8 2 ♘h6 mate.

And now let us examine some mating attacks on the castled position with rook and knight.

Here White lands a double blow on a7 – **1 ♘c6+ ♚a8 2 ♖xa7 mate**.

1 ♘e7+ ♚h7 2 ♖h5 mate

In the final position (*see diagram next column*) White first traps the king by **1 ♖d8+**, and after **1...♚g7** he shuts it in with **2 ♘f6**, after which mate by **3 ♖g8** cannot be avoided.

Of course, there are numerous possible mating finishes, and we have given only the most elementary, which you would do well to remember: they will occur time and again in your games, and will serve as reliable guides when carrying out a mating attack on the enemy king.

13 Mating Attack Mechanisms

The coordination of the forces becomes clearly apparent in a mating attack, and so let us try to establish how a mating mechanism is created and how it works. We will begin with the following schematic position.

The black pieces are huddled around their leader, and seem to be ready to parry any attack on it. A check on the diagonal can be blocked by rook, bishop or knight, and a check on the file also by rook, bishop or knight.

But by **1 Rh5+** White puts the black king in double check, and it transpires that the king has to move. But where to? The numerous defenders, crowding around the king, are occupying the g7 and g8 squares, to

where it might retreat. And it turns out that White's rook and bishop, by coordinating their actions into a double blow, aimed at the black monarch, give mate, whereas the army of black pieces, and there are no less than seven of them, not only do not help, but even prevent the king from moving out of the firing line.

But what if in the previous position there was no knight at g8, and this square were free?

In this case too Black cannot defend against the attack. After **1 Rh5+ Kg8** White gives mate by **2 Bh7**.

Of course these two positions present exceptional situations, in which the black pieces are particularly uncoordinated, but sometimes in the course of a game this lack of coordination among the opponent's forces can be created, as in the following position.

Chudinovskikh–Zhuravlev
USSR 1990

White's heavy pieces are impending over the black king, but how is he to continue the attack? After all, Black is threatening to take the rook at h6, and then to play his knight to d3, neutralising the opponent's light-square bishop.

If you look deeply into this position, and compare it with the previous one, you will probably find the correct solution. White gives mate in four moves as follows:

1 **Xh8+!** ♘xh8 **2 Wh7+!** ♔xh7, and now, exactly as in the previous example, 3 **Xh5+** and 4 **♗h7 mate**.

By sacrificing his rook and queen, White not only destroyed the coordination of the black pieces, but also created the conditions for the successful implementation of a double blow.

Let us consider another schematic position.

Black's forces are elegantly deployed on three sides around their king, but the d5 square on the d-file is not covered, and by 1 **Xd5** White gives mate.

And in the following schematic position, where the black knights are absent, their role is taken over by a second white rook.

Here, as in the previous example, White gives mate by **1 ♖d5**.

Such a mate by two rooks, with the remaining pieces deployed in the most varied ways, occurs quite often in practice.

A classic example of such a linear mate is provided by the conclusion to the following game.

Schmid–Hofman
Germany 1958

In reply to **1 ♖h6+** the black king is obliged to run to the defence of its rook at c7, and this plays a fatal role.

1...♔e7 2 ♖g7+ ♔d8 (or 2...♖f7 3 ♖xf7+ ♔xf7 4 ♖xh7+, winning the rook) **3 ♖d6+ ♔c8 4 ♖g8+**, and mate next move.

In the following two examples a mating attack is combined with the striking of double blows.

(*see diagram next column*)

To defend against the mate by the queen at f6, Black played **1...♕d4**,

but then White carried out his second threat – **2 ♕xh7+ ♔xh7 3 ♖h1+** and mate next move.

Ivanov–A.Petrosian
USSR 1978

Note that 1...♗g6 would not have saved the game: 2 ♖xg6 hxg6 3 ♕xg6, and, since the rook at e8 is under attack, there is no satisfactory defence against 4 ♖h1 mate.

Miles–Uhlmann
Hastings 1975/6

After **1...♕xh2+ 2 ♔xh2 ♖h6 3 ♕e8 ♘f6** White resigned.

The following game demonstrates an example of mutual chess blindness.

Barcza–Tarnowski
Szczawno Zdroj 1950

Here White played **1 f5?**, over-looking that by 1...♕f3+! his opponent could force mate. But Black too did not see this mate. He replied **1...♖g3**, and in the end he even went on to lose.

A spectacular linear mate was found by Black in the following game (*see diagram next column*).

White is threatening mate in one move, and at first sight there appears to be no satisfactory defence. However...

1...♕h4+!! 2 gxh4

If White takes on h4 with his king, he is immediately mated by 2...♖xh2.

2...♖e3+ 3 ♗f3 ♗xe6+! 4 ♕xe6 ♖xf3 mate

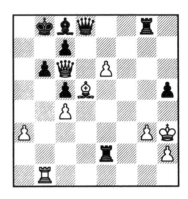

Osloukhov–Nedobora
USSR 1990

Superb, wouldn't you agree?

Let us sum up. As you will have seen, in mating mechanisms the placing of the opponent's pieces and pawns is often exploited. After all, for the king it is quite immaterial which pieces are hindering it, its own or the enemy pieces; it is important only that they restrict the space available to it. By the skilful exploitation of the enemy forces, the number of attacking pieces in a mating attack can be reduced to the minimum.

It should also be noted that in a mating attack there are solo pieces, which fulfil the main role, and there are also secondary pieces, but the choice of actors on the chess stage belongs to you. The former play an active role, the latter a largely passive one, but even the latter should not be underestimated: without their participation the mating mechanism would not work. Figuratively speaking, in a mating mechanism there are moving parts, but also non-moving. And it is the role of the latter that is played by the opponent's pieces and pawns.

14 Combinations and Sacrifices

On many occasions you yourself have probably noticed that situations on the board frequently occur where, in reply to the purposeful actions of one of the players, the replies of the other are forced. He is essentially obliged to go along with the idea of the opponent, and is unable in any way to change the inexorable course of events. The pieces and pawns of both sides are as though linked with one another by invisible threads, and, obeying the will of one of the players, they whirl around like puppets performing a ritual death dance.

Such situations are usually called combinations. The results of a combination can be very varied – mate to the king, winning of material, obtaining a positional advantage, gaining equal chances, or finally, attaining a draw.

Several definitions of a combination have been suggested, but we will not go into all these theoretical subtleties. It is important only to mention that a combination is nomally forcing and leads to a definite aim. It should be added that often, especially in the middlegame, an accompanying, although not obligatory, feature of a combination is a sacrifice.

We already know that in tactical play the opponent's pieces and pawns can be forced to help our aims. This is achieved in the most varied ways, but the strongest and most effective of these is the sacrifice. Usually it appears suddenly and unexpectedly, and comes as an unpleasant surprise to the opponent. The suddenness and unexpectedness of a sacrifice is due to the fact that we usually make use of the comparative values of the pieces, which apply in normal situations. When we are still studying the rudiments of chess, we learn that a queen is much stronger than a rook, that a rook is stronger than a bishop or knight, and that the latter are much stronger than a pawn.

Such truths are firmly lodged in our mind. We know, of course, that these correlations are not something inflexible, but in practice we often forget this. However, in tactical positions, where there is a wealth of attacks and threats, these correlations are, to a significant degree, arbitrary. Very often the strength of a particular piece at a given moment is determined by its degree of participation in the tactical operation in progress. If for the success of a mating attack the defences around the opponent's king have to be destroyed, we do not begrudge giving up material, since in the end it will be regained with interest. It is the same with a double blow. If it brings us material gain, then for it to occur we can also give up something. The only problem is that we first have to give up something, and then regain it.

Therefore in a sacrifice an element of risk is always present: suppose that the opponent somehow manages to wriggle out and the sacrifice proves incorrect? This means that a sacrifice normally requires precise and sometimes deep calculation. In the end everything has to be weighed up.

Sacrifices can be used to achieve the most varied tactical aims, but in particular they serve as a means of disorganising the opponent's defences or fully eliminating them.

It often happens that our forces are already coordinated against some target, but for the success of the operation we need to reduce or fully eliminate the defensive resources. It is this aim that is provided by a sacrifice. This and the following examples show how this is done.

Here White played **1 ♖xf6!**

On 1...♔xf6 there follows 2 ♗xg5+, while if 1...♕xf6 2 ♘h5+. Black's seemingly solid position collapses, and so he conceded defeat.

As you see, by the sacrifice of his rook White lures the black king to f6. This is known as a luring or **decoy sacrifice**. In the given example, with the help of a luring or decoy sacrifice White carried out a simple double blow combination.

Fischer–Gligoric
Zagreb 1970

Here, by threatening mate – **1 ♕h6**, White forces the reply **1...♖g8**, and then, by sacrificing his queen for the h7 pawn covering the king, **2 ♕xh7+!**, he destroys Black's defences, and after **2... ♔xh7** gives mate by **3 ♖h2**.

This is an example of a **destructive sacrifice**, the aim of which was to eliminate the defences of the enemy king.

Here White gives mate in three moves:

1 ♗f8+! ♗h5 2 ♕xh5+! gxh5 3 ♖h6 mate

This is an example of a **diverting sacrifice**. By giving up his queen for the bishop at h5, White diverts the g6 pawn which is covering the h6 square against the penetration there of the white rook, as a result of which this mating finish becomes possible.

Thus the elimination of defenders or their disorganisation can usually be achieved by means of three types of sacrifices – decoy, destructive and diverting. However, sacrifices can fulfil not only a destructive role, but also a constructive one, by assisting the necessary coordination between the attacking pieces and the target of the attack.

White gives mate in two moves: **1 ♖e8+! ♔xe8 2 ♕e7 mate**

By a decoy sacrifice he co-ordinates the actions of queen and knight with the target of the attack – the black king, creating the required mating mechanism.

Karpov–Csom
Bad Lauterberg 1977

It sometimes happens that a player's own pieces prevent the carrying out of a combination, and hinder the required coordination of the forces. Naturally, such pieces can well be given up, by sacrificing them.

Thus here, were it not for his knight at g3, White would have 1 ♕h2+ ♔g8 3 ♕g3+, forcing mate.

He therefore played 1 ♘f5!, and Black resigned.

After 1...♘xd7 2 ♕h2+ ♔g8 3 ♕g3+ he is again mated, while 1...♘h4 allows 2 ♖h7+ ♘xh7 3 ♕g7 mate.

Thus we have met another type of sacrifice – for the vacating of a square. A sacrifice can also be made for the vacating of a line, if some piece is preventing another piece from fulfilling especially important functions on this line. The following example demonstrates this situation.

Manov–Hairabedian
Bulgaria 1962

If the bishop were removed from h5, and also the rooks from d8 and g8, then by ...♕h8 Black would be able to force mate. This means that these pieces must be eliminated:

1...♗e2! 2 ♕xe2 ♖h8+ 3 ♔g1 ♖h1+! 4 ♔xh1 ♖h8+ 5 ♔g1 ♖h1+! 6 ♔xh1 ♕h8+ 7 ♔g1 ♕h2 mate

Such a sacrifice, which has the aim of vacating a square or line, can be called a **vacating sacrifice**.

Ormos–Betatski
Budapest 1951

Here Black's position looks critical, but if we notice that his king does not have a single move, we easily find a series of sacrifices leading to stalemate and a draw.

1...♖b1+ 2 ♔h2 ♖h1+! 3 ♔xh1 ♘g3+!

The knight has to be taken, otherwise the queen will be lost.

4 fxg3 ♕xg2+!

The final sacrifice, which puts everything in its place. After **5 ♔xg2** Black is stalemated!

It is time to take stock. We have established that sacrifices can serve the aim both of disorganising or eliminating the opponent's defences, as well as, on the contrary, assisting the coordination of our own forces. These sacrifices can be very varied.

We have established that there are five basic types of sacrifices:

1. The decoy sacrifice, when the opponent's pieces or pawns are lured onto some definite squares.

2. The diverting sacrifice, when the opponent's pieces or pawns are diverted from fulfilling some important functions.

3. The destructive sacrifice, when pieces or pawns destroy the opponent's defences.

4. The vacating sacrifice, when pieces or pawns are sacrificed to vacate squares or lines, needed for the actions of our pieces.

5. The self-eliminating sacrifice, when pieces or pawns are simply unnecessary or superfluous. They prevent the attainment of some aim, and must be removed from the board.

In practice, all these types of sacrifices occur in pure form, but it is more usual for a sacrifice to pursue simultaneously several aims.

In the following position, by sacrificing his queen White gives mate in two moves:

1 ♕c6+! dxc6

Or 1...♗xc6.

2 ♘a6 mate

This sacrifice, firstly, lures the pawn (or bishop) to c6, depriving the king of this square, and secondly, it simultaneously vacates the a6 square for the knight to land the mating blow.

Thus this is an example of the combination of a diverting and vacating sacrifice.

P.Romanovsky, 1950

Here too White gives mate in two moves, by sacrificing his queen.

1 ♕f8+! ♖xf8 2 ♘e7 mate, or
1...♔xf8 2 ♖h8 mate.

By this sacrifice White either lures the rook to f8, diverting it from the defence of e7, or lures the king to the same square, diverting it from the control of h8. This means that this is an example of a decoy and diverting sacrifice.

Gogolev–Varshavsky
Aluksne 1967

Things look hopeless for Black, but he saves the game with the help of two sacrifices.

1...♖d3+! 2 ♕xd3

The acceptance of the sacrifice is forced: after 2 ♔g4 ♕d1+ White even loses.

2...♕e3+! 3 ♕xe3 – stalemate!

What kind of sacrifices were these? The first, by the rook at d3, was of course self-eliminating, but at the same time it kept the white queen in the vicinity of the e3 square, i.e. it was also effectively a decoy sacrifice.

The second sacrifice is especially interesting. By giving up his queen, Black not only eliminates it, but simultaneously lures the white queen to e3, thereby pinning the g5 pawn and creating the fortunate possibility of a stalemate. This means that here we have an

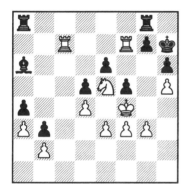

Alekhine–Yates
London 1922

Here White carries out an operation involving a knight sacrifice:

1 ♘d7 ♔h8 2 ♘f6! ♖gf8 3 ♖xg7!

By giving up his knight, White destroys the opponent's defences, while simultaneously luring the black rook to f6.

3...♖xf6 4 ♔e5!

This king move crowns matters: 4...♖ff8 or 4...♖af8 allows mate in two moves by 5 ♖h7+ and 6 ♖cg7.

Black therefore resigned.

example combining decoy and self-eliminating sacrifices.

It should be mentioned that in a single combination, albeit a fairly complicated one, virtually all types of sacrifices may sometimes be encountered.

Korchmar–Polyak
Kiev 1937

All the white pieces are threateningly impending over the enemy king, Black's position hangs by a thread, and it is not surprising that White finds a spectacular combination, demonstrating the veracity of an old saying – a chain is as strong as its weakest link!

Let us try to find this combination. It is not hard to see that Black's central defender is his knight at d6. Were it not for the knight, White would give mate in three moves by 1 ♖e8+ ♖f8 2 ♖xg7+ and 3 ♖xf8.

In turn, if the white knight were not at d5, 1 ♕xd6 would be

possible, eliminating the important black knight. Therefore the initial moves of the combination are easy to find:

1 ♘b4! axb4 2 ♕xd6! ♕d7

The first wave of the attack is over, and Black's last move is his only defence. But how is White to continue the attack? Exploiting the fact that the black queen is tied to the defence of the e8 square, White finds a second queen sacrifice:

3 ♕d5!!

The queen cannot be taken on account of 4 ♖e8+, and meanwhile White is threatening to capture on g7, since the rook at f7 is pinned. Black has nothing better than **3...♔f8**, but then White for the third time sacrifices his queen: **4 ♖xg7! ♕xd5**, and now he nevertheless gives mate: **5 ♖g8+! ♔xg8 6 ♖e8+ ♖f8 7 ♖xf8 mate**.

Let us investigate what happened here. By 1 ♘b4 White eliminated his knight. This was a vacating sacrifice, opening the d-file for his queen. 2 ♕xd6 was a destructive sacrifice: an important defender of the black king had to be removed.

The prettiest move in the combination was undoubtedly 3 ♕d5. This – a diverting sacrifice – is an attempt to divert the black queen from the defence of e8. Incidentally, if Black had replied to this not with 3...♔f8, but 3...g6, then 4 ♖ge3, with the unavoidable penetration of the rook to e8, would have been decisive.

The rook capture on g7 is a combination of a destructive and a decoy sacrifice: after 4...♖xg7 the reply 5 ♕xd7 becomes possible.

Finally, the last sacrifice, 5 ♖g8+, is an example of a decoy-diverting sacrifice: the black king that is lured to g8 is diverted from the defence of the e8 square.

Thus in this combination four types of sacrifice are present – vacating, destructive, diverting and decoy.

In studying the different types of sacrifices, we have largely examined only those that comprise parts of a combination. Such sacrifices are essentially temporary, bringing an advantage at the finish of the combination. Certain authors altogether regard them as 'pseudo-sacrifices': after all, in the end they are fully repaid.

However, there are sacrifices that are of a completely different character, and which are repaid by no means immediately. In particular, these are sacrifices for the initiative, for a lead in development, in order to hinder the development of the opponent's pieces, and so on. Such sacrifices are customarily called 'real'. All that they give are some advantages, which only later, and by no means by force, may bring some appreciable gains. Real sacrifices are most often of a strategical nature: they are normally associated with the subsequent plan, although they may lead to tactical complications and combinations.

Real sacrifices occur most frequently at an early stage of the game. For example, in the King's Gambit, Evans Gambit, the Chatard-Alekhine Attack against the French Defence, the Morra Gambit against the Sicilian Defence, the Scotch Gambit, and in many other sharp opening lines.

15   Classification of Combinations

There is no need to demonstrate that the combination is one of the most interesting elements of the game of chess, but, at the same time, also one of the most complicated. And, like any complicated phenomenon, it may be characterised in various ways.

Using the aims of combinations it is easy to divide them into two large groups – those in which one of the side wins, and those in which a draw is attained. These are customarily called **winning combinations** and **drawing combinations**.

Such a division looks perfectly logical – firstly, it defines the aim of a combination, and secondly, it allows the inclusion of studies, which, as is known, are demarcated precisely in this way. As regards the further division of combinations, we consider it advisable to do this depending on the targets at which they are aimed, and on the arrangement of the forces arising at the end.

Depending on the target of the attack, winning combinations can be clearly divided into three groups. The first includes those in which the target of the attack is the king, the second – combinations against all the remaining pieces, and the third –

combinations in which the theme is the promotion of a pawn. Since the latter largely occur in the endgame, we will barely touch on them here.

Combinations against the king can be divided into three sub-groups, depending on the type of attack. In the first sub-group will be combinations ending in mate, and those in which the mate is parried, but at the cost of great material loss. The main point here is that the king is subjected to a combined attack, where one piece attacks the king and others restrict it, not allowing it to escape by fleeing.

The second sub-group includes combinations associated with a double blow, where a threat of mate is combined with some other strong threat or attack. Such combinations do not lead to mate, but end with the defending side suffering unbearable material losses. Finally, to the third group we assign combinations with a double blow, where the king is merely one of the two targets of attack. In this case there is no threat of mate, but only an attack on the king.

The classification of winning combinations, when the target of attack is the king, is shown in the accompanying table.

		Mating combinations (combined attack on the king)
		Double blow, including the threat of mate
	Combinations against the king	Double blow, including an attack on the king
WINNING **COMBINATIONS**	**Combinations to win material**	Combined attack on a piece or pawn
		Double blow
	Combinations to promote a pawn	Simple promotion of a pawn
		Double blow, including the threat of promoting a pawn

DRAWING **COMBINATIONS**	Perpetual check
	Stalemate
	Blockade
	Perpetual pursuit
	Fortress
	Drawing balance of forces

Combinations to win any of the other pieces can logically be divided into two sub-groups. The first covers those, at the finish of which the win of material is accomplished by a combined attack, i.e. when the piece is attacked and simultaneously it is not allowed to escape.

The second sub-group covers double blow combinations, in which an attack on a piece is combined with some other threats or attacks, apart, of course, from attacks or threats to the king.

The arrangement of combinations to win material is also presented in the table.

Combinations to promote a pawn can be divided in similar fashion. In one group will be combinations, in which the threat of promoting a pawn leads either to the appearance of a new queen, or to decisive material losses for the opponent. And in the other sub-group will be combinations, in which the threat of promoting a pawn is combined with other strong threats to or attacks on a piece.

All these types of winning combinations are given in the table, as are drawing combinations, which can be divided into six sub-groups. Combinations leading to perpetual check (on the king) and to perpetual pursuit (on any other piece) are typical of the middlegame, whereas combinations leading to stalemate, the blockade of some important enemy piece, the construction of a fortress, or the reduction to a drawing balance of forces are more typical of the endgame, but are nevertheless worth knowing.

16 Winning Combinations

Thus, as regards the target of the attack, winning combinations have been divided into three groups. The first covers combinations directed against the king, the second covers combinations against the other pieces and pawns, and the third covers combinations to promote a pawn.

We will now separately examine combinations in each of these groups.

Combinations against the king

The first in this group are mating combinations, at the conclusion of which a mating mechanism operates and mate is given.

Radulov–Sederborg
Helsinki 1961

White's queen, rook and two bishops are aiming threateningly at the kingside. In order to get at the enemy king, he needs to deprive it of its pawn screen. This is achieved by a rook sacrifice, which here both destroys the opponent's defences and also lures his king into a pin.

1 ♖xg7! ♔xg7

The rook has to be taken: 2 ♖xh7+ or 2 ♗xf6 was threatened.

2 ♕g4+ ♔h8 3 ♕h5

Note should be made of a highly significant subtlety – the moves by the queen to g4 and h5 became possible, only because Black's king was lured onto the diagonal of the bishop at e5. The mating mechanism – queen, supported by the other bishop, attacking h7 – has already been created. The bishop at e5 is also indirectly participating in it, by paralysing the knight at f6. Mate cannot be prevented: on 3...♔g8 there follows 4 ♗xf6 ♖fe8 5 ♕xh7+ ♔f8 6 ♕h8 mate.

Kopayev–Averbakh
Leningrad 1946

Here the white king has come out in front of its pawn screen, and in addition its defenders are on the opposite wing. Not surprisingly, it immediately comes under a strong attack, since Black can quickly open the h-file.

1...h4 2 ♕c3+ ♔d7 3 ♕e5

At full steam the white queen hastens to the aid of her sovereign, but it is already too late...

3...hxg3+ 4 ♔xg3 ♖h3+!

The rook is sacrificed in order to set up a mating mechanism. The king is lured to the fatal h3 square and diverted from the defence of f3, for where the black queen is aiming.

5 ♔xh3 ♕f3+ 6 ♔h4 ♗e7+

Here we see a queen giving mate in conjunction with a bishop, with the queen merely fulfilling a restricting role, the honour of landing the decisive blow going to the bishop. White has nothing better than 7 ♕g5, but after 7...♕xf4+! 8 ♔h3 ♕xg5 the game is over. This example differs from the preceding one, only in that, at the cost of heavy material loss, mate can be averted, which, however, does not affect the result.

Mating combinations may also be associated with a double blow, when a threat of mate is combined with some less strong threat or attack. Such combinations normally lead to a win.

Here is a typical example of such a combination:

Parr–Wheatcroft
London Championship 1938

By **1 ♖h5!** White landed a spectacular double blow. The black queen is attacked, but if **1...♕xd7** there follows mate in two moves – **2 ♘g5+ ♔h8 3 ♖xh6 mate**.

It is worth mentioning once again that such combinations, involving a double blow, often arise suddenly and unexpectedly. At any event, for one of the players!

Here is a characteristic example:

Solovyev–Averbakh
Moscow 1945

Here Black's pieces are the more actively placed, although at first sight there is nothing to suggest that the end is close for White. In fact his position is critical: his queen is severely restricted, and Black is able to exploit this factor.

1...♘e2+ 2 ♔f1 ♘f4 3 ♕h7

It appears that Black can win immediately by 3...♕e6, threatening mate in three moves (4...♕e2+ 5 ♔g1 ♕xe1+), but White parries this threat by 4 ♕e4, and after 4...♕xe4 5 dxe4 Black cannot play 5...♖xe4 on account of 6 ♖d8 mate.

Black's correct reply is **3...♕f7!**

The white queen is trapped, and does not have a single square to go

to. And meanwhile Black is threatening 4...♘g6, finally locking the dungeon door, and then 5...♖h8, wining the queen.

To defend against this threat, White has to resort to extreme measures.

4 ♖c1 ♘g6 5 ♗g3 c6

To 5...♖h8 White was intending to reply 6 ♖xc7+ ♕xc7 7 ♕xg6.

6 ♖c5

On 6...♖h8 White was planning 7 ♖f5, but Black has available a deadly double blow, prepared far in advance, which immediately decides the game.

6...♗c3!

On the one hand the queen is attacked, and on the other hand mate is threatened at e1. Therefore White resigned.

And now a double blow combination, in which the king is simply one of the targets attacked.

Botvinnik–Menchik
Hastings 1934/5

Black's position is difficult. Trying to exchange the strong white bishop, which is aiming at e6 and f7, she played **1...♗d5**, and this is what happened:

2 fxe6 ♗xb3 3 e7+!

A little, but highly effective combination. By this pawn sacrifice the black king is lured into a double blow. After 3...♔xe7 4 ♘c6+ White's material advantage is sufficient for a win, and so Black resigned.

Combinations to win material

Combinations of this type are divided into two groups. The first covers combinations in which the win of a piece is achieved by a combined attack on it, i.e. when an attack on this piece is made, and it has no possibility of moving away, or of defending against the attack. The second sub-group concerns double blow combinations, where the attack on a piece is combined with attacks or threats of attacks on other pieces.

A typical example of a combined attack is given in the following diagram.

Here White played **1 f5**.

After the pawn capture 1...♖xd4 he was intending to reply 2 fxe6 ♗xe6 3 ♗xe6 fxe6 4 ♘g6 ♖e8 5 e5 ♘fd5 6 ♕f2, with a double blow – an attack on the rook and the threat of a check at f7.

Botvinnik–Stepanov
Leningrad 1934

Therefore Black replied **1...exf5**, assuming that the d-pawn would not run away. But in fact this move was a mistake, allowing White to carry out a combination against the black queen.

There followed **2 ♗xf7+! ♖xf7 3 ♘c4**, and the queen was trapped.

Novotelnov–Rovner
Moscow 1946

This is an example of a combination to win a piece by a double blow.

White was apparently satisfied with his position: the b6 pawn is attacked, and 2 f6 is threatened. But it was Black's turn to move and, seizing on a significant defect in the placing of the opponent's pieces (poorly defended back rank), he unexpectedly sacrificed a piece:

1...♗xf5! 2 ♗xf5 ♘xf5 3 ♖xf5 ♖ed8!

A very important move in Black's plan – now the queen has to retreat, such that it is simultaneously guarding the back rank.

4 ♕c4 ♖ac8 5 ♕e2 ♖xc2 6 ♕xc2 ♕c8!

Let us try to investigate what happened. By a piece sacrifice Black first lured the white rook to f5 and diverted it from the defence of the back rank. Then the white queen was lured to c2. All this has led to a double blow – with its last

move the black queen has attacked the opponent's queen and rook. White is helpless: he can neither take the queen, nor defend the rook, and on 7 ♖f2 there follows 7...♕xc2 8 ♖xc2 ♖d1 mate.

Combinations to queen a pawn

It is clear that the advance of a pawn and its promotion to any piece, but especially to a queen, is an effective method of gaining a material advantage. In the middlegame such situations occur comparatively rarely. We give an exceptional example, where a pawn became a queen immediately after the opening.

Larsen–Spassky
Belgrade 1970

---

1 b3 e5 2 ♗b2 ♘c6 3 c4 ♘f6 4 ♘f3 e4 5 ♘d4 ♗c5 6 ♘xc6 dxc6 7 e3 ♗f5 8 ♕c2 ♕e7 9 ♗e2 0-0-0 10 f4

White has played the opening in original style, but this has not done him any good: Black has successfully completed the mobilisation of his forces and is ready to begin active play. And White's last move is a serious mistake, which merely assists the opponent.

10...♘g4! 11 g3 h5 12 h3 h4!

By sacrificing a piece, Black mounts an irresistible attack on the white king.

13 hxg4 hxg3 14 ♖g1

Now comes an unexpected sacrifice that assists the advance of the pawn and opens the h4-e1 diagonal for the black queen.

14...♖h1! 15 ♖xh1 g2 16 ♖f1

There is nothing better; if 16 ♖g1 ♕h4+ 17 ♔d1 ♕h1! 18 ♕c3 ♕xg1+ 19 ♔c2 ♕f2, and White can resign.

16...♕h4+ 17 ♔d1 gxf1=♕+ 18 ♗xf1 ♗xg4+

White resigns; after 19 ♗e2 he is mated next move.

Of course, combinations to promote a pawn that involve a double blow are also possible.

The first impression in the following position is that Black stands badly – his knight is lost. However, the seemingly harmless, but strong passed c3 pawn enables him to sacrifice his knight, but carry out a winning combination.

Weltmander–Polugayevsky
Sochi 1958

1...♘g3+!

With this sacrifice Black opens the f-file for the following double blow.

2 fxg3 ♕f6+ 3 ♕f2

There is nothing else: otherwise White loses his rook.

3...♖xe1+ 4 ♔xe1 ♕xf2+ 5 ♔xf2 c2, and the pawn queens.

It is useful to investigate the mechanism of this double blow. 2...♕f6+ is a double attack (on the rook and the king), in combination with the latent threat of promoting the pawn to a queen.

17 Drawing Combinations

We will begin our examination of drawing combinations with those in which the target of the offensive is the king, but where the attack on the monarch leads not to mate, but to perpetual check.

Perpetual check

This situation arises most often when the enemy king's defences are destroyed, but there is insufficient force to give mate. In the majority of cases, attacks on the king leading to perpetual check are carried out by the queen. The following is a classic example:

Alekhine–Em.Lasker
St Petersburg 1914

Here Lasker played **1...h6**, with the aim of determining the position of White's dark-square bishop. But the advance of the pawn seriously weakens the king's fortress, a factor that Alekhine exploits with two destructive sacrifices.

2 ♗xh6 gxh6 3 ♖xe6 fxe6 4 ♕g3+ ♔h8 5 ♕g6

White's queen, also supported by his bishop, has ended up dangerously close to the black king. But Black's knight is securely covering h7, and it turns out that White is unable to create mating threats.

After **5...♕e8** all that he has is perpetual check: **6 ♕xh6+ ♔g8 7 ♕g5+ ♔h8** (of course, not 7...♔f7 8 ♕g6 mate) **8 ♕h6+**, and the players agreed a draw.

Sometimes perpetual check may be a way to save the game, after an attack has petered out.

Smyslov–Vasyukov
Moscow 1961

The first impression is that White's attack has come to a halt, and that he cannot avoid loss of material. But there is a way to save the game:

1 ♖h5+!

This destructive sacrifice exposes the king, which proves sufficient for perpetual check.

1...gxh5 2 ♕d6+ ♕g6 3 ♕f8+ with a draw.

A threat of perpetual check may be combined in a double blow with some other strong threat, for example, a threat of mate.

Ryumin–Verlinsky
Leningrad 1933

Black's strong passed pawn at d2 gives him the advantage, but by threatening mate White manages to draw the game by perpetual check.

1 ♖f1! d1=♕ 2 ♕e6+! ♔h7
(2...♕xe6 3 ♖f8+ ♔h7 4 ♖h8 mate)
3 ♘f8+ ♔h8 (3...♕xf8 4 ♕g6+ ♔g8 5 ♕e6+) **4 ♘g6+** with a draw.

Stalemate

Stalemating combinations occur rather rarely in the middlegame, and are much more common in the endgame. In most cases stalemate occurs when one side, with a significant material advantage, and where the win is within reach, overlooks the opponent's defensive resources.

Here is one of the best known examples of this type.

Evans–Reshevsky
New York 1963

It is patently clear that White stands badly. He is a piece down, his king is in mortal danger, and it seems time to resign. However, Evans did not resign, but made a move that his opponent evidently took to be a gesture of despair.

1 h4! ♖e2+ 2 ♔h1 ♕xg3

Anticipating immediate capitulation, Reshevsky did not take the trouble to clarify his opponent's intentions, and captured the pawn (he should have played 2...♕g6 3 ♖f8 ♕e6!). But now White's king has no move, and he needs only to get rid of his superfluous queen and rook.

There follow two self-eliminating sacrifices:

3 ♕g8+! ♔xg8 **4 ♖xg7+**, and the capture of the rook leads to stalemate, while if it is not taken, then the 'desperado' rook gives perpetual check.

Stalemate is usually the last saving chance. But this is by no means a straw at which a drowning man clutches. The threat of stalemate is a very real defensive procedure, which should always be kept in mind.

Taimanov–Geller
Moscow 1951

White's position is lost: against the numerous threats there is no defence. The game lasted just three more moves:

1...♖xh2 2 ♕e3 ♖a8 3 ♖g7+

A gesture of despair, which Black simply ignored.

3...♔h6, and White resigned.

Later it was established that with his first move Geller had let slip the win. 1...♖g4! was correct, e.g. 2 ♖h3 ♖c1+ 3 ♔e2 ♖g2+ and 4...♖c3 mate.

Taking the pawn with 1...♖xh2 allowed Taimanov the possibility of an elegant stalemating combination – 2 ♖xg8 ♔xg8 3 ♖g3+!

This decoy sacrifice, which is simultaneously self-eliminating, deprives the white king of any moves. After the forced 3...♕xg3 the king is stalemated, and White only needs to get rid of his queen – 4 ♕b8+ ♔g7 5 ♕g8+! with a draw.

Blockade

It is well known that in an attack the pieces should support one another, so that their actions against the enemy king are coordinated. Therefore when there is a small number of attacking pieces, a system of defence is possible, based on shutting one of these pieces out of play.

(*see diagram next page*)

The black pawn cannot be prevented from queening, but it turns out that even in this apparently quite hopeless position White has a possibility of saving the game.

V.Chekhover, 1954
(*conclusion of a study*)

after **F.Simkhovich**, 1924
White to play and draw

He plays **1 ♗g4!**

This move constitutes a typical double blow. On the one hand White attacks the pawn, and, if Black takes the bishop – 1...♔xg4, then after 2 f3+ and 3 ♔f2 the king stops the pawn and the draw becomes completely obvious.

And in reply to **1...e1=♕** White carries out his second threat – by **2 h3!** he completely shuts in the black king at h4, after which the queen alone is unable to do anything.

It is not only the king that can be blockaded, but any other piece, even the queen. Thus in the following position Black's king, together with his bishop, is securely shut in the corner, but his queen is threatening to break out to freedom, after which the white pawns, like ripe apples, will fall one after another. But White succeeds in blocking in the queen.

1 d4! ♕d8 2 h4, and, despite Black's enormous material advantage (extra queen), he is unable to win.

Such a method of defence is not often encountered, but it is nevertheless worth knowing.

Perpetual pursuit

With perpetual check it is the king that is pursued, but other pieces too can be subjected to such a continuous attack. Although this theme is one that has been thoroughly developed by study composers, it also occurs occasionally in practice. The following position shows one such example.

Black's pieces are scattered, and his queen is practically shut out of the game. In addition, e4-e5 is threatened. However, the congested placing of the white pieces on the kingside allows Black to carry out a combination on the theme of perpetual pursuit.

Zurakhov–Bukhman
Kiev 1967

1...♗g4 2 hxg4

After 2 ♕f2 ♗xe2 3 ♘xe2 ♕xf2+ Black has nothing to fear.

2...♘xg4 3 ♖fe1

Since the h1 square is defended by the knight, the attack by queen and knight against the white king is not so dangerous. But what proves decisive here is the fact that the white queen is very restricted in its movements, and Black is able to begin a pursuit of it.

3...♘h2! 4 ♕f2 ♘g4 5 ♕f3

The only move: after 5 ♕f1 White is mated.

5...♘h2 with a draw.

Fortress

The construction of an impregnable fortress, into which the opponent's pieces are unable to penetrate, is an important strategical method of defence.

Flohr–Lilienthal
Budapest 1950

White has a queen for rook and pawn, but the play is all on one wing, and the result depends on whether or not he can take the opponent's fortress by storm.

There followed **1...♘f5! 2 ♗xf5**

Flohr thought that after this exchange he would easily win with his passed pawn, but the resulting position constitutes an impregnable fortress. 2 ♕f4 was stronger, so as then to try to break up Black's defences by the advance of the h-pawn.

2...gxf5 3 ♔g2 f4 4 h4 ♔h7 5 ♔f3 ♖e3+ 6 ♔xf4 ♖e6 7 ♔f5 ♖g6 8 h5 ♖h6 9 ♔g5

White's pieces have approached right up to the opponent's defences, but they are unable to penetrate inside the fortress.

9...♖e6 10 ♕d8 ♔g7

The queen cannot be allowed to go to f8.

11 ♕d4+ ♔h7 12 ♕h4 ♖h6 13 ♕b4 ♔g7 14 ♕b8 ♖e6 drawn.

The idea of constructing a fortress is not always obvious. Sometimes it can be highly camouflaged.

V.Chekhover, 1947
White to play and draw

White has three pawns for the exchange, and his task does not appear difficult. But outward impressions can often be deceptive. Black has the dangerous threat of invading the opponent's position and capturing a couple of pawns, after which it will not be difficult for him to win.

For example: 1 ♔c2 ♖h2 2 ♗f1 ♖xf2 3 ♗d3 ♖g2, or 1 ♗f3 ♖f8 2 ♗d1 ♖xf2 3 g4 ♖g2 4 ♔c2 ♖g3, and, by taking his king to e4, Black wins.

Thus we can conclude that the loss of even one pawn on the kingside will signify defeat.

What then can White do? Does he have any possibility of avoiding the loss of any pawns? It turns out that he has, and a very unusual one – he must give up his bishop!

Initially this idea looks pointless, but the paradox is that, thanks to this seemingly quite incomprehensible piece sacrifice, White succeeds in evicting the rook from his position and in setting up an impregnable fortress.

1 ♔d1! ♖h2 2 ♔e1 (or 2 ♔e2) **2...♖xg2 3 ♔f1 ♖h2 4 ♔g1 ♖h6 5 f3! ♖e6 6 ♔f1 ♔f7 7 ♔f2**

A unique position has arisen. Black is a rook up, but here it proves impossible to exploit this advantage. White has set up a pawn barricade, and his king is securely guarding all the entrances and exits.

And in conclusion – a humorous study on the theme of the fortress.

A.Rudolph, 1912
White to play and draw

The task of making a draw may cause perplexity: White's position looks completely hopeless. But he does not lose heart:

1 ♗a4+!!

What nonsense! As it is, White has so little force, and he gives up another piece.

1...♔xa4 2 b3+ ♔b5 3 c4+ ♔c6 4 d5+ ♔d7 5 e6+ ♔xd8

If the pawns are disregarded, the white king has to battle alone against a hugely superior enemy force, but after **6 f5**, permanently locking the fortress, Black is powerless to invade the enemy position, and is unable to realise his enormous material advantage. Therefore – draw.

Drawing balance of forces

Such combinations, like the preceding ones, occur most often in the endgame. The following ancient example is typical.

G.Greco, 1623
Black to play and draw

Black is two pawns down, but he nevertheless saves the game by an exchanging combination:

1...♖a1+ 2 ♖f1 ♖xf1+ 3 ♔xf1 ♗h3!

In this way, by giving up his bishop for the g-pawn (or to transform the g-pawn into an h-pawn after 4 gxh3), Black achieves a well-known theoretical position, in which White's extra bishop does not give him a win.

In the following, more complicated example, White achieves a drawing balance of forces by means of a double blow.

(see diagram next page)

White is rook down. In order to gain a draw he must save his knight and win the enemy bishop.

M.Perelman, 1955
White to play and draw

1 e7 ♖e4+ 2 ♔f1! ♖xe5 3 ♘c7! ♖xe7 4 ♘d5!

An extremely effective move, which constitutes a double blow. The knight attacks the rook and simultaneously carries the threat of a double attack on king and rook. Therefore the black rook cannot move to e8, e6 or e4.

4...♖e5

The only move. But now White carries a second order threat.

5 ♘f4+ ♔g4 6 ♘d3, with a double attack on rook and bishop.

18   Chess Aesthetics

For anyone who knows nothing about chess, the little pieces are nothing more than wooden or plastic knick-knacks. It is hard to believe that they are capable of living a complicated life, full of dangers. But man's thinking and imagination inspire these pieces, and they, like real actors, are capable of giving wonderful performances. These may be tragedies, dramas, or even comedies. And what is most interesting is that the person moving these pieces, and also any spectator present, himself becomes a direct participant in the performance. He does not know what the outcome of the spectacle will be, and he experiences excitement, surprise, delight, frustration and despair, since the seemingly unpretentious pieces are capable, as it turns out, of touching the most sensitive and innermost parts of the human soul. And it is then that a game of chess is transformed into a work of art, which not only gladdens the mind, but also warms the heart.

Among the feelings accompanying the struggle on the chess board, the strongest and most profound is undoubtedly the feeling of beauty – beauty of idea, beauty of human thought. This beauty acts with unusual intensity on our imagination.

No one is surprised therefore by the enthusiastic applause of the spectators, when some game is concluded by a spectacular, deeply calculated combination.

And it becomes understandable why, in the majority of chess events, special prizes are awarded for brilliancy, and the most beautiful games and combinations find their way into publications throughout the world.

But what is meant by a beautiful game or a beautiful combination?

In order to answer this question, we will acquaint you with a few combinations from the treasury of chess art, the most striking masterpieces of chess creativity.

Zukertort–Blackburne
London 1883

Black's kingside is weakened, but he is pinning all his hopes on his knight move to e4. However, White simply disregards this threat, having seen that he will later gain excellent attacking possibilities.

1 f5!

When playing this, Zukertort would have had to calculate accurately all the consequences.

1...♘e4 2 ♗xe4 dxe4 3 fxg6!

Played with Olympian calm: White is not afraid of 3...♖c2.

3...♖c2 4 gxh7+ ♔h8 5 d5+ e5

White's attack appears to have come to an end. That, at any event, is evidently what the commander of the black pieces thought, but it is here that the full depth and beauty of Zukertort's idea is revealed. He sacrifices his queen!

6 ♕b4!! ♖8c5

Alas, the acceptance of the sacrifice leads to a forced mate – 6... ♕xb4 7 ♗xe5+ ♔h7 8 ♖h3+ ♔g6 9 ♖g3+, and the reader himself can

establish that, after bringing his second rook into play, White gives mate in a few moves. But the move played also does not save Black. A new sacrifice follows:

7 ♖f8+! ♔xh7

If 7...♕xf8 8 ♗xe5+ ♔xh7 9 ♕xe4+ ♔h6 10 ♖h3+ with a quick mate.

8 ♕xe4+ ♔g7 9 ♗xe5+! (another rook sacrifice) **9...♔xf8 10 ♗g7+!!**

A spectacular concluding stroke! 10...♕xg7 allows 11 ♕e8 mate, while if 10...♔xg7 11 ♕xe7+. Black therefore resigned.

The beauty of Zukertort's combination consists in the series of spectacular sacrifices – queen, rook (twice) and bishop, but the most beautiful move, of course, was the initial and quite unexpected queen move to b4. No less important is the fact that the combination arose as a result of a clash of ideas.

Steinitz–Bardeleben
Hastings 1895

The situation looks rather complicated and unclear: Black is a pawn up, and is threatening, after exchanging rooks, to win the knight. It is true that White has available a discovered check with his knight, but what does it lead to?

1 ♘g5+ ♔e8 2 ♖xe7+!

It begins! It is bad for Black to take the rook with his queen on account of the obvious 2...♕xe7 3 ♖xc8+ ♖xc8 4 ♕xc8+, while if he takes it with the king, then 2...♔xe7 3 ♖e1+ ♔d6 4 ♕b4+ ♔c7 (4...♖c5 5 ♖e6+) 5 ♘e6+ ♔b8 6 ♕f4+ ♖c7 7 ♘xc7 ♕xc7 8 ♖e8 mate.

Such a combination is not difficult to calculate, and if that was all there was to it, it would hardly merit distinction. But the fact that White's rook at c1 has been left undefended allows Black to make a paradoxical move, prepared beforehand. In this way he was hoping to refute White's idea.

2...♔f8!

A quite worthy reply. 'Go ahead,' the black monarch seems to be saying, smiling ironically, 'take my queen if you want, and you will be mated on the back rank!'

Surely White wasn't like the hunter in the old Russian fairy tale, who caught a bear, but the trouble was, the bear wouldn't let him go!

However, it transpires that Steinitz had also anticipated this.

3 ♖f7+!

Very clever: the rook is still immune.

3...♔g8 4 ♖g7+!

Nothing short of miraculous! The rampant rook feels perfectly at home in the enemy position.

4...♔h8

There is simply nothing else. 4...♔f8 is decisively met by 5 ♘xh7+.

5 ♖xh7+!

Here the game concluded, and what's more, rather unexpectedly. Realising that he was losing, the stunned Bardeleben could not hide his feelings, and was so upset that he got up from the board, left the playing hall, and... did not return. He was, of course, awarded a loss.

The unsporting behaviour of his opponent did not allow Steinitz to conclude his brilliant combination, the finish to which he promptly demonstrated:

5...♔g8 6 ♖g7+ ♔h8 7 ♕h4+! ♔xg7

White's efforts have been crowned by success – he has finally forced his opponent to accept the rook sacrifice. But now the black king comes under a series of deadly blows by the queen and knight.

8 ♕h7+ ♔f8 9 ♕h8+ ♔e7 10 ♕g7+ ♔e8

After 10...♔d6 11 ♕xf6+ White gives mate next move.

11 ♕g8+ ♔e7 12 ♕f7+ ♔d8 13 ♕f8+ ♕e8 14 ♘f7+ ♔d7 15 ♕d6 mate

The beauty of this truly grandiose combination lies not only in the fact that it extends for 14 moves, involves the repeated sacrifice of a rook, and ends in a spectacular mate. Perhaps the most important thing is that Steinitz anticipated the paradoxical king move, on which his opponent was pinning all his hopes.

In the following position White's defences in the centre, under fire from all sides by Black's long-range pieces, look decidedly shaky. The question is, how to demolish them?

Rotlewi–Rubinstein
Lodz 1907

Possible here was the prosaic 1...♘xh2 2 ♕h5 ♗xe4 3 ♘xe4 ♘xf1, or 2 ♗xb7 ♘xf1 with the threat of 3...♘g3+. But the line chosen by Black is, of course, far more beautiful and spectacular.

1...♕h4 2 g3

Stumbling into the main variation of the combination. Now the black pieces, like a pack of hungry wolves, fall on the enemy monarch.

2...♖xc3!! 3 gxh4 ♖d2!!

A fantastic position! Black has given up his queen, and four of his pieces are en prise, but the capture of any of them leads to mate or to irreplaceable loss of material.

If 4 ♗xc3 ♗xe4+ 5 ♕xe4 ♖xh2 mate, or 4 ♕xg4 ♗xe4+ 5 ♖f3 ♖xf3 6 ♕g2 ♖f1+ 7 ♖xf1 ♗xg2 mate. Finally, 4 ♗xb7 is met by 4...♖xe2 5 ♗g2 ♖h3! 6 ♗xh3 ♖xh2 mate.

That only leaves the line chosen by White.

4 Wxd2 Bxe4+ 5 Wg2 Rh3

White resigns, since there is no defence against the mate at h2.

Here, of course, the queen sacrifice was very fine, and the position arising after it extremely striking, but all the play was in one direction: White could do nothing to oppose the powerful enemy blows.

Incidentally, it is worth seeing how Black's attack would have developed, if White had defended with 2 h3 instead of 2 g3.

Here Black even has two ways to win. One is combinational, where the variations are not so spectacular as after 2 g3, although they are convincing enough.

2...Bxc3! 3 Bxc3

The best reply. A forced mate results from 3 Wxg4 Rxh3+! 4 Wxh3 Wxh3+! 5 gxh3 Bxe4+ 6 Bh2 Rd2+.

3...Bxe4 4 Wxg4

After 4 Wxe4 Wg3! 5 hxg4 Wh4+ White is mated.

4...Wxg4 5 hxg4 Rd3! 6 Bh2

The only defence against 6...Rh3 mate.

6...Bxc3, and with two bishops for a rook Black must win this ending.

However, the second, totally prosaic way, is even simpler – 2...Bxe4 3 Nxe4 Ne3! 4 Rfc1 (there is no other defence against 4...Bc2) 4...Wxf4, with a material advantage.

Adams–Torre
New Orleans 1920

Outwardly the position looks quiet, and so after **1 ♗xf6**, without especially considering the consequences, Black replied **1...♗xf6**, although 1...gxf6 came into consideration. The point is that in this case 2 ♖xe7 does not work on account of 2...♕xe7! (but not 2...♖xe7 3 ♖xe7 ♕xe7 4 ♕g4+ and 5 ♕xc8).

After the capture with the bishop, Black's queen is tied to the defence of the rook at e8, which allows White to carry out a wonderful combination.

2 ♕g4! ♕b5!

It turns out that Black too has powder left in his keg! In moving out of the attack, the queen in turn creates the threat of capturing on e2.

3 ♕c4!!

A worthy reply! The queen is untouchable. It not only defends the rook at e2, but itself threatens to take the opponent's queen, which has to retreat.

3...♕d7 4 ♕c7!!

Miraculous! The queen again offers itself, but due to the mate threat it cannot be taken in either way.

4...♕b5 5 a4!

This move – the sacrifice of an insignificant pawn – is no less strong than the preceding queen sacrifices. In a combination everything is identically important – sacrifices, attacks, and even the most simple moves.

Incidentally, without this important move White's combination would not have worked: on the immediate 5 ♕xb7 Black can reply 5...♕xe2!

5...♕xa4 6 ♖e4! ♕b5 7 ♕xb7!

The triumph of the attack! The black queen perishes on the field of battle. Black resigns.

In this combination the four queen sacrifices are spectacular, of course, but I think that the subtle move 6 ♖e4! is no less pretty. After all, in combination with the pawn sacrifice at a4, it is only this move that makes the entire combination correct and leads to a win.

(*see diagram next page*)

Black has just captured a white knight at h5, assuming that after 1 ♕xh5 f5 he would have time to erect a defensive line. Therefore, without losing time on regaining the piece, White immediately destroys the fortifications in the vicinity of the opponent's king.

Lasker–Bauer
Amsterdam 1889

1 ♗xh7+! ♔xh7 2 ♕xh5+ ♔g8 3 ♗xg7!! ♔xg7

The second sacrifice has to be accepted. If 3...f6, then 4 ♖f3 ♕e8 5 ♕h8+ ♔f7 6 ♕h7.

4 ♕g4+ ♔h7 5 ♖f3 e5

Only in this way can Black prevent the threatened mate.

6 ♖h3+ ♕h6 7 ♖xh6+ ♔xh6

For the moment Black has quite adequate compensation for the queen – a rook and two bishops. But the following move, which had to be seen in advance, puts everything in its place: White wins a further piece.

8 ♕d7! ♗f6 9 ♕xb7, and White won.

Lasker's combination, involving the sacrifice of both bishops, became a classic, and has been repeated many times in practice. The bishop sacrifices are spectacular, but their effectiveness depended on the final double blow.

You have seen just a few of the dazzling ancient combinations from the treasury of chess art. I hope that you liked them. In fact, the golden fund of chess contains many more, and modern tournaments are constantly adding fresh examples.

All the given combinations are characterised by originality of thought, spectacular, deeply calculated sacrifices, and paradoxical moves that are difficult to find – everything that in chess constitutes beauty.

But I should like to emphasise one further important feature of the chess combination. A game of chess is a clash of two personalities, and this means two intellects and two characters, and an artistic chess production is created in the course of the struggle between them.

For this reason, even a spectacular combination that is unexpected for one of the sides, where the play is all in one direction and one of the players is given the role of a whipping-boy, by the laws of chess beauty must be valued much less than one where there is a clash of ideas, when both players go in for one and the same position, but one sees a little further, when one sees a combination, and the other sees its refutation. If from this viewpoint we examine the examples given, the combinations in the Zukertort-Blackburne and Steinitz-

Bardeleben games should be rated more highly than, say, the combinations in the Rotlewi-Rubinstein and Lasker-Bauer games.

As an example of such a clash of ideas, I should like to give the following ending:

Averbakh–Zita
Szczawno Zdroj 1950

As can be seen, the position is extremely sharp. Black's king has no pawns covering it, but as yet it is not evident how it can be attacked. White's king is comparatively safe, but the central black pawns are ready to rush forward. Who will be the first to create real threats?

1 ♕f5 d3 2 ♖f4 d2+ 3 ♔d1 e3

Just three moves have been made, and the white king is in mortal danger: there appears to be no defence against 4...e2+. Thus 4 ♖e4

is met by the decisive 4...e2+ 5 ♖xe2 ♕xe2+! 6 ♔xe2 d1=♕+ and wins. And on 4 ♖g4+ my opponent had prepared the spectacular reply 4...♖g6, when after 5 ♖xg6 hxg6 6 ♕xg6+ (6 h6+ ♔h7) 6...♗xf8 Black is a rook up.

Why then did White nevertheless go in for this continuation? Because he saw in advance a refutation of the opponent's combination!

The game concluded:
4 ♖g4+ ♖g6 5 h6+!

This modest pawn move radically changes the situation, by opening the h-file for an attack by the white queen. Black has only one reply:

5...♔xh6 6 ♖xg6+ hxg6 7 ♕h3+!

Now it all becomes clear. After both 7...♔g5 8 ♕h4, and 7...♔g7 8 ♕h8 there is only one outcome – Black is mated.

19   Strategy of Attack

Up till now we have been examining situations in which the warring forces have already made contact, and tactics have come to the fore. We will now turn to a study of positions in which the main feature is strategy, where if the forces of the two sides have come into contact, then only in the centre, and the subsequent actions demand the drawing up of a correct plan that corresponds most closely to the features of these positions. It should be mentioned that the choice of plan depends to a certain extent on the pawn structures of the two sides, but to an even greater degree it is determined by where the main target of the attack is located – the enemy king.

Depending on the placing of the kings, four typical situations can be distinguished:

(a) One or both kings are deprived of the right to castle or are unable to castle.

(b) Both kings have castled on the kingside.

(c) The kings have castled on opposite sides.

(d) The kings have both castled on the kingside, but the offensive is mounted on the queenside.

We will now examine what will be the strategy of attack in each of these cases.

Attack on the uncastled king

At the very start of a game the players have to solve the problem of the safety of their kings. Since in the majority of openings the position is usually opened in the centre, they aim to take their kings as far away as possible from the fighting that begins in the centre, and castle either on the kingside, or on the queenside. Only in exceptional cases, when the centre is blocked, and play is conducted on the flanks, may a player try to gain time for developing his initiative, economise on castling and not hurry to evacuate his king from the centre.

In certain openings a player will endeavour to deny the opponent's king the right to castle, and for this will be prepared to sacrifice material. Here we will examine several instances, where for some reason one of the kings is caught in the centre and becomes a target for attack.

Our task is to establish how in such positions the offensive actions are planned, and how the attack is conducted.

As a rule, in open positions with an uncastled king it is extremely dangerous to begin active play. The following example convincingly demonstrates this.

Averbakh–Estrin
Moscow 1964

White has a clear lead in development, yet, tempted by the win of a pawn, Black risks beginning active play: **1...♗xc3+ 2 ♕xc3 ♘xe4**

He does not fear 3 ♗b5+ on account of 3...♘c6. But...

3 ♘b5! ♕c5

Black assumed that the attack on f2 would gain time for the defence.

4 ♕xg7! ♖f8 5 ♗h6 ♕xf2+ 6 ♔d1 ♘d7

Thus both kings have lost the right to castle. But White's forces are fully mobilised, and this allows him to make an immediate assault on the enemy monarch, whereas his own king in the middle of the board feels completely safe.

7 ♖e1!

Less clear is 7 ♘c7+ ♔d8 8 ♘xa8 ♕c5!, with two threats – 9...♕xc4 and 9...♘f2+.

7...♘ef6

If 7...♘ec5, defending the e6 pawn against attack, then 8 ♗e3! ♕h4 9 ♘d6+, winning the queen.

8 ♗xe6! ♕xb2

The bishop cannot be taken on account of mate in two moves.

9 ♖c1

What can Black do now? 9...♕xb5 is met by 10 ♗c4+, and meanwhile White is threatening 10 ♗xd7+ ♔xd7 11 ♖c7+ ♔d8 12 ♕xf8+, mating. There is no defence against this, and so Black resigned.

Tal–Fuster
Portoroz 1958

Black has delayed evacuating his king from the centre, and now queenside castling can be answered by 2 ♘xf7, and kingside castling by 2 g5.

He therefore played **1...f6**, having decided first to drive away the knight, and then nevertheless to castle queenside. The loss of the e6 pawn did not worry him: in return he was intending to pick up the g3 pawn. However, in order to hold the opponent's king in the centre, White sacrificed a piece.

2 ♗xe6! fxe5 3 dxe5 ♗e7

After 3...♗xe5 4 ♖he1 White's attack is too dangerous. For example: 4...♗xg3 5 ♗d7+ with a quick mate, or 4...♗f6 5 ♗c8+ ♔f7 6 ♕e6+ ♔g6 7 h5+ ♔g5 8 ♕e3+ with mate to follow.

4 ♖hf1

Threatening 5 ♗f7+ ♔f8 6 ♗g6+ ♔g8 7 ♕c4 mate.

4...♖f8 5 ♖xf8+ ♗xf8 6 ♕f3!

Black is tied hand and foot. For example, he cannot play 6...♖d8 because of the simple 7 ♖xd8+.

6...♕e7 7 ♕b3

Threatening 8 ♗d7+ ♕xd7 9 ♖xd7 ♔xd7 10 ♕xb7+ and 11 ♕xa8.

7...♖b8?

This loses quickly. The toughest defence was 7...b5, e.g. 8 ♗d7+ ♕xd7 9 ♖xd7 ♔xd7 10 ♕f7+ ♗e7 11 e6+ ♔d6 12 ♕xg7 ♗e4 13 ♕xh6 ♗d5, and Black can still hold on.

8 ♗d7+! ♕xd7 9 ♖xd7 ♔xd7 10 ♕f7+ ♗e7 11 e6+ ♔d8

11...♔d6 would have been answered by 12 ♕f4+, winning the rook.

12 ♕xg7

Black resigns. After 12...♗e4 13 ♕e5 he loses his bishop.

The possibility of opening up the position is an important factor in evaluating positions with an uncastled king.

Flohr–Simagin
Moscow 1945

Black did not like the fact that, if he castled, his opponent would play his bishop to a3 and a rook to e1, winning a pawn and retaining the initiative. Therefore he played **1... ♔d7**, thinking that his powerful pawn group in the centre would safeguard his king against attacks. But with two energetic blows White destroys the black fortress.

2 c4 dxc4 3 d5!

This pawn sacrifice, which Black is obliged to accept, completely exposes his king.

3...♘xd5 4 ♖d1

The position has radically changed: only fragments remain of Black's pawn defences, and 5 ♖xd5+ is threatened. His next move is practically forced, but, faced by the opponent's heavy pieces, his king, strolling about in the centre of the board, immediately finds itself in danger.

4...♔e6 5 ♕xc6+ ♕d6 6 ♕xc4 ♖ad8

6...c6 is decisively met by 7 ♗f4, e.g. 7...♕d7 8 ♕e4+, and mate follows in two more moves.

7 ♕g4+ ♔e7 8 ♕xg7 ♔d7

The king tries to flee from its pursuers, but in vain.

9 ♗g5 ♖df8 10 ♕d4 c6 11 ♗f4 ♕a3 12 ♕e5

Black resigns: if 12...♖c8 there follows 13 ♖xd5+ cxd5 14 ♕xd5+ ♔e8 15 ♖e1+ etc.

Averbakh–Goldberg
Tula 1955

The weakening of the opponent's pawn structure allows White to open lines by a piece sacrifice and to begin an immediate attack on the king.

1 exf5 gxf5 2 ♘xf5! exf5 3 ♖e1!

First and foremost the king must not be allowed to castle.

3...d6

There is nothing better. If 3...h6, defending against 4 ♗g5, there would have followed 4 ♗f4 ♕d8 5 ♘d5 ♘xd5 6 ♕h5+ ♔f8 7 ♗xd5 with a decisive attack. 3...♘c6 also does not help on account of 4 ♗f4 ♕a5 5 ♘d5 ♘xd5 6 cxd5. Finally, 3...♔d8 can be met by 4 ♖xe7! ♔xe7 5 ♗g5 with numerous threats.

4 ♗g5 ♔d8

4...♔d7 is met by the decisive 5 ♖xe7+, while if 4...♔f7 5 ♘d5.

5 ♖xe7! ♕xe7 6 ♘d5 ♘xd5

Black gives up his queen, but this does not delay the end for long.

7 ♗xe7+ ♘xe7 8 ♕xd6+ ♘d7 9 ♖d1!

A curious position! Black has no way of defending against the capture on b7, after which he inevitably loses material.

9...♖g8 10 ♗xb7 ♖g6 11 ♕d4 ♘c6 12 ♕b6+ ♔e8 13 ♗xc6 Black resigns

Attack on the kingside

By castling on the kingside, the king comes under the protection of its pawns. But even behind such a pawn screen it may be subjected to an attack, if the opponent succeeds in creating a significant advantage in force on the kingside.

Averbakh–Fridstein
Vilnius 1946

Here White played **1 ℞d3**, intending to swing the rook across to g3 or h3, to attack the enemy king. Black should have forestalled the opponent's plan by 1...e5, forcing the queen to go to e3.

Instead of this he replied **1...b5**, beginning an attack on the queenside, which, however, came too late. There followed:

2 ℞g3 (threatening to take on f6) **2...♚h8 3 ℞h3!**

The most vulnerable target for White's attack is the h7 pawn. The knight that is defending it is attacked by the bishop at g5, and so for the success of the operation it is sufficient for him to attack h7 a second time. The decisive 4 e5 dxe5 5 ♕h4 is already threatened.

3...♕b7

Black parries the threat with a double attack on g2. Now 4 e5 is refuted by 4...♝xg2+ 5 ♚g1 ♝xh3.

The position has become sharper, and combinations are in the air. White includes his second rook in the attack.

4 ℞f4!

It turns out that he does not have to fear 4...e5: he replies 5 ℞fh4!, and if 5...exd4 6 ♝xf6 with inevitable mate.

What can Black do now? The hanging positions of the opponent's pieces suggest to him a counter-combination.

4...♘xe4

This unexpected continuation sets White difficult problems. To 5 ♘xe4 Black was intending to reply 5...♝xe4, attacking g2 and gaining time for the defence: if 6 ♝xe7 there follows 6...♝xg2+ 7 ♚g1 ♝xh3, threatening mate.

If instead 5 ♝xe7, Black was intending to play 5...♘xc3, threatening to win the queen by 6...♝xg2+ 7 ♚g1 ♘xe2+.

And yet White fell in with his opponent's plans! Why?

5 ♝xe7 ♘xc3

The reason was that in his calculations he had foreseen a spectacular way of immediately deciding the game in his favour.

Look at the diagram position. The black king is defended only by pawns, and in White's attack there are four pieces (queen, both rooks and bishop). All he needs to do is break up the royal fortress, since the king on its own will be unable to withstand the opponent's superior forces. And the role of destroyer is played by none other than the queen.

6 ♕xg7+! ♔xg7 7 ♖g4+ ♔h8 8 ♗f6 mate

The power of White's attack is demonstrated by the fact that he could even have managed without his rook at f4, and still given mate in six moves – 7 ♖g3+ ♔h6 8 ♗g5+ ♔g7 9 ♗xd8+ ♔h6 10 ♗g5+ ♔g7 11 ♗e7+ ♔h6 12 ♗xf8 mate.

If the attacker is able to concentrate his pieces on the kingside, the attack will normally be very dangerous. The following example is typical.

The basic drawback of Black's position is that on his kingside 'all the doors and windows are open', and this decides the battle in favour of White: unhindered, he can launch an assault on the royal fortress.

Kotov–Unzicker
Stockholm 1952

1 ♖e4 ♘f8 2 ♘f5 ♔h8 3 ♕h5

'White's play is simple,' wrote grandmaster Kotov regarding this game. 'As many pieces as possible on the kingside. Black has no way of opposing this.'

3...♖c7 4 ♖h4

Only four moves have passed, and White has created such an advantage in force on the kingside, that there is already no defence. There is the threat of a knight sacrifice at g7 or h6.

4...♘h7 5 ♘xg7! ♔xg7 6 ♗xh6+ ♔g8 7 ♖g4+ ♖g6 8 e6!

Black resigns. 8...♖xg4 is met by 9 ♕xg4+, and meanwhile 9 exf7+ is threatened.

Of course, in the position just considered Black had no counterplay, and the white pieces were able to storm the king's fortress without hindrance. This is by no means always the case. Often the opponent's defences have to be broken up, which may demand considerable effort.

Alekhine–Colle
Bled 1931

White's bishops are aimed at the kingside, which creates the necessary preconditions for an attack. It is true that, in order to obtain this position, White has sacrificed a pawn.

1 ♖ab1 ♖d8
Defending against the threat of 2 ♗b4.
2 ♖e3
The rook is ready to swing across to g3.
2...b6 3 ♕e2
If immediately 3 ♖g3, then 3...♘h5 4 ♖g4 ♘f6.
3...♗b7 4 ♖g3 ♘e8
The exchanging combination 4...♖xd3 5 ♕xd3 (stronger than 5 ♗xf6, which is also possible) 5...♗e4 does not work on account of 6 ♖xg7+! ♔xg7 (6...♔f8 7 ♕g3)

7 ♕xe4, with a decisive advantage.
However, 4...♖ac8 was stronger. Black incorrectly goes totally onto the defensive, which makes things markedly easier for White.
5 ♖e1 ♔f8 6 ♕b2!
White exploits the opponent's mistake by provoking an important weakening of his pawn structure.
6...f6 7 ♗b4 ♘d6 8 ♖ge3 ♔f7
If 8...e5 9 f4.
9 f4 ♕d7 10 ♕e2!
Simultaneously creating two threats – 11 ♖xe6 and 11 ♕h5+ followed by the penetration of the queen into the enemy position.
10...♖e8 11 ♕h5+ ♔g8 12 ♕g6 f5 13 ♗xd6 ♕xd6 14 ♗xf5 ♕xf4 15 ♕h7+ ♔f8 16 ♗g6 ♕d4 17 ♗xe8 ♖xe8 18 ♔h1 ♕f6, and Black resigned.
The finish could have been 19 ♕h8+ ♔f7 20 ♕xe8+ ♔xe8 21 ♖xe6+.

Averbakh–Fuchs
Dresden 1956

An attack on the kingside may arise suddenly, as a result of events occurring in the centre or even on the queenside.

Thus here the rook at a3 is in a position to swing across to the kingside, but as yet it is not clear how this can be carried out. At the same time Black is threatening to attack the queenside pawns by 1...♘e5 or 1...♕b4. Incidentally, he is also inviting the opponent to begin complications after 1 ♗e7 ♘e5. But White has quite different plans.

1 ♘e4!

Unexpectedly the black queen begins to feel uncomfortable: 2 ♗d2 is threatened. In addition, the d6 pawn is hanging. Against 1...♘e5 White had prepared the following combination, in which the decisive role is played by the rook at a3 – 2 ♕h3! ♘bxc4 3 ♘f6+ ♗xf6 4 ♗xf6 ♘d7 (otherwise there is no defence against the threat of 5 ♕h6) 5 ♕xh7+! ♔xh7 6 ♖h3+, and mate next move.

1...♘c8 2 ♕h3! ♕c7 3 ♕h4 ♖e8

There is nothing better. If 3...f6 4 ♖h3 h5 5 ♗xh5 fxg5 6 ♘xg5 gxh5 7 ♘e6 ♕b6 8 ♘xg7 ♔xg7 9 ♕xh5 with a decisive attack.

4 ♖h3 h5 5 ♘g3!

White has no reason to hurry, and so he prepares the sacrifice on h5. The immediate 5 ♗xh5 would not have succeeded on account of 5...♖xe4! 6 ♕xe4 gxh5 7 ♖xh5 ♘f8.

5...♘f8 6 ♗xh5 ♗xb2

If 6...gxh5 7 ♘xh5 ♘g6 8 ♘f6+ ♗xf6 9 ♗xf6 ♘xh4 10 ♖xh4 with inevitable mate.

7 ♘f5! gxh5

If Black takes the knight – 7...gxf5, then 8 ♗f6 ♗xf6 9 ♕xf6 is possible, and if 9...♕e7 10 ♗xf7+! ♕xf7 11 ♖h8 mate.

8 ♗f6 ♘g6 9 ♕g5 ♘ce7 10 ♘h6+ ♔f8 11 ♗xb2 Black resigns

To launch an attack on the kingside one often has to resort to a pawn storm, the aim of which is to open lines for attacks by the heavy pieces.

Botvinnik–Zagoryansky
Sverdlovsk 1943

The forces of both sides are grouped around the isolated black pawn – White's pieces are attacking it, and Black's are defending it. Exploiting the fact that the opponent's pieces are markedly restricted, Botvinnik begins a pawn attack on the kingside. The fact that, in so doing, he exposes his own king, does not worry him: the opponent's pieces are fully occupied with the defence of the d5 pawn.

1 g4! ♛c6 2 g5 hxg5 3 ♛xg5 f6 4 ♛g6 ♝f7

The capture on h3 would have been too risky, since it would have allowed White quickly to switch his rooks to the h-file.

5 ♛g3 f5 6 ♛g5 ♛e6 7 ♚h1

At the cost of creating new weaknesses (the f5 pawn), Black has included his queen in the defence and for the moment has prevented White from doubling heavy pieces on the h-file. But now for this aim White uses the g-file.

7...♛e5 8 ♖g1 ♖f8 9 ♛h6 ♖b8 10 ♖h4

White has after all achieved his aim. His queen penetrates into the enemy position.

10...♚f8 11 ♛h8+ ♝g8 12 ♖f4!

A shift of fire! The rook has helped the queen to invade the opponent's fortress, and now it begins besieging the f5 pawn.

12...♖bb7

Black covers in advance his vulnerable g7 point.

13 ♖g5 ♖f7 14 ♛h5

The triumph of White's plan. He has shattered the opponent's kingside defences, broken into his position, forcing the black pieces to take up uncomfortable positions, and then attacked the weak f5 pawn with superior forces. It cannot be defended, and the game does not last long:

14...♛a1+ 15 ♚h2 g6 16 ♛xg6 ♝h7 17 ♛d6+ ♖be7 18 ♛d8+ Black resigns

If the opponent's pieces are fairly active, an attack by the pawns from in front of the king may prove double-edged, by opening lines for the invasion of the enemy pieces. In such cases, before beginning the pawn storm, the player should try to evacuate his king to a safer place, usually on the opposite wing.

Attack after castling on opposite sides

As we have seen, if the kings have castled on the same side, an attack is mainly carried out using the pieces. Pawns take part comparatively rarely in such an attack, more as an exception.

It is a quite different matter after castling on opposite sides. Here the offensive is mainly carried out by pawns. It is normally they that are sacrificed for the sake of opening lines for the heavy pieces or with the aim of breaking up the enemy fortress. Since both sides can engage in such a pawn storm, it is very important to be able to outpace the opponent, in order to be the first to reach the main target of the attack – the enemy king.

It should be mentioned that if any of the pawns in front of the castled king have moved, this makes it easier to storm the king and to open lines. And pieces too, standing in the path of the pawns, can facilitate their advance.

We will begin with an example where White carried out a pawn storm without any difficulty.

Alekhine–Marshall
Baden Baden 1925

1 f4 ♕e6
If 1...♕a5 2 e5, and 2...♘d5 can be met by 3 ♘xd5 ♗xd5 4 ♗xh7+ ♔xh7 5 ♕d3+ and 6 ♕xd5.

2 e5 ♖fe8 3 ♖he1 ♖ad8
By pinning the e5 pawn, Black tries to restrain the pawn offensive, but not for long.

4 f5 ♕e7 5 ♕g5 ♘d5 6 f6
The fact that the black knight and queen were in the path of the pawns has born fruit – White's pawns have already come into contact with the opponent's pawns.

6...♕f8 7 ♗c4!
The position has become sharper, and White finds a tactical solution.

7...♘xc3 8 ♖xd8 ♖xd8 9 fxg7!
♘xa2+ 10 ♔b1!

This is the whole point! After 10 ♗xa2 Black would have had a saving check at c5.

10...♕e8 11 e6!
Simpler than 11 ♗xf7+, which would also have won.

11...♗e4+ 12 ♔a1 f5
There is no way of saving the game. 12...fxe6 is met by 13 ♗xe6+ ♕xe6 14 ♕xd8+ ♔xg7 15 ♕d4+ and 16 ♖xe4.

13 e7+ ♖d5 14 ♕f6 ♕f7 15 e8=♕+ Black resigns

Spassky–Petrosian
Moscow 1969

Black is ready to play ...b7-b5, but White is the first to begin a pawn storm.

1 g4! ♘xg4
If 1...b5 there could have followed 2 g5 hxg5 3 fxg5 ♘h5 4 g6! fxg6 5 ♕g5. In order to maintain his pawn screen, Petrosian decides to accept the pawn sacrifice.

2 ♕g2 ♘f6 3 ♖g1 ♗d7 4 f5!
♔h8

By allowing lines to be opened, Black goes down without a fight. 4...e5 was the lesser evil.

5 ♖df1 ♕d8

Returning the queen to the defence, but 5...♕e5 was the toughest defence. Now, however, White's attack develops swiftly.

6 fxe6 fxe6 7 e5! dxe5 8 ♘e4 ♘h5

Probably the only move. 8...exd4 can be met by 9 ♘xf6 g5 10 ♕h3 ♖e7 11 ♖xg5 with a decisive attack.

9 ♕g6! exd4

An obvious mistake. More tenacious was 9...♘f4, and if 10 ♖xf4 exf4 11 ♘f3 ♕b6, planning after 12 ♘f6 to give up queen for rook. In this case White would have had to find the decisive move 12 ♖g5!

10 ♘g5! Black resigns

If 10...hxg5 11 ♕xh5+ ♔g8 12 ♕f7+ ♔h8 13 ♖f3, and there is no defence against the mate.

Fischer–Spassky
Belgrade 1992

In order to outpace the opponent in the development of his attack, Black is offering the b4 pawn, reckoning on 1 ♕xb4 to reply 1...♗c6 followed by 2...♖b8, with active play on the queenside. However, Fischer finds the 'Achilles' heel' in Black's set-up.

1 ♘b6!

It is extremely important for White to exchange his badly placed knight.

1...♖b8

1...♘xb6 would have been met by 2 ♕xb4, and if 2...d5 3 ♕xb6 ♕xb6 4 ♗xb6, when 4...dxe4 is bad on account of 5 ♖d7, winning a piece.

2 ♘xd7 ♕xd7 3 ♔b1 ♕c7 4 ♗d3 ♗c8 5 h5

After completing his development and placing his pieces on the required squares, White begins a pawn storm.

5...e5 6 ♗e3 ♗e6 7 ♖dg1 a5 8 g6! ♗f6

8...f6 is met by the decisive 9 h6!, e.g. 9...hxg6 10 ♖xg6 ♖f7 11 hxg7 ♖xg7 12 ♕h2! ♗f8 13 ♖xf6 etc.

If instead 8...fxg6 9 hxg6 hxg6, then after 10 ♕h2 ♔f7 11 ♕h7 White has a very strong attack.

9 gxh7+ ♔h8 10 ♗g5

Naturally, White aims to exchange an important defender of the royal fortress.

10...♕e7

The queen hurries to the aid of the bishop, but 10...♗xg5 11 ♖xg5 f6 would perhaps have been a tougher defence.

11 ♖g3 ♗xg5 12 ♖xg5 ♕f6 13 ♖hg1 ♕xf3

In search of counter-chances. Otherwise after 14 ♕g2 the g7 pawn all the same cannot be defended.

14 ♖xg7 ♕f6 15 h6 a4 16 b3

Forestalling possible attempts at counterplay.

16...axb3 17 axb3 ♖fd8 18 ♕g2 ♖f8 19 ♖g8+!

White's task is a simple one – he needs to eliminate both of his h-pawns, which are covering the opponent's king against checks on the file.

19...♔xh7 20 ♖g7+ ♔h8 21 h7!

Black resigns. There is no defence against the threat of 22 ♖g8+ ♔xh7 23 ♖h1+ ♕h6 24 ♕g7 mate.

Averbakh–Petrosian
Moscow 1961

In this position White can regain his pawn with 1 ♕xc4, but he considered it more important to begin a pawn storm immediately.

1 g4! ♘bd7 2 f4 ♕a5 3 f5!

In positions such as these, pawns do not have to be counted – the main thing is to be able to expose the opponent's king. After 3...exf5 4 gxf5 ♘xe4 White was intending 5 fxg6 ♘xc3 6 gxh7+, and if 6...♔xh7 7 ♕c2+, or 6...♔f7 7 ♕f3+, regaining the piece.

3...♖ab8

Petrosian aims at all costs to gain counterplay, and the situation becomes extremely sharp.

4 fxg6 hxg6 5 e5 ♖xb2

After 5...dxe5 6 ♕c2! the game would have quickly concluded, whereas now White must defend accurately to avoid, in turn, coming under a crushing attack.

6 ♔xb2

After 6 ♕xb2 ♖b8 Black answers 7 ♕a1 with 7...dxe5, while if 7 ♕c2 he wins the queen by 7...♕a3+ 8 ♔d2 ♖b2.

6...♖b8+ 7 ♔c2 ♘d5 8 ♕xc4 g5

Threatening 9...♘e3+.

9 ♖d3 ♘b4+ 10 ♔d1 d5 11 ♕b3 c5

Or 11...♘xd3 12 ♕c2 ♘7xe5 13 dxe5 ♗xe5 14 ♕xd3 ♕xc3 15 ♕g6+ ♗g7 (15...♔h8 16 ♗g7+ ♗xg7 17 ♘xg5+ with a quick mate) 16 ♕xe6+ ♔h8 17 ♗xg7+ ♔xg7 18 ♕e7+ ♔g8 19 ♕xg5+, and White wins.

12 ♕b1 c4 13 ♕c1 Black resigns

It is useful to know the following standard attacking procedure, which has occurred many times in practice.

Averbakh–Sarvarov
Moscow 1959

Black appears to have been the first to begin his attack, but this impression is erroneous: his offensive has no specific aim, whereas White's pawn storm involves a concrete tactical blow.

1 ②e5 ②b7 2 g4 a5 3 ③dg1 a4 4 g5 ②h5 5 ③xh7+!

This is the point! This sacrifice wins by force.

5...②xh7 6 g6 fxg6 7 ♕xg6

Unexpectedly, four white pieces, headed by the queen, have ended up close to Black's monarch. He has only one reply:

7...②7f6 8 ♕f7+ ③h8

If 8...③h7 the following pretty variation was possible: 9 ③g6! ②g8 10 ③xg7+ ②xg7 11 ♕g6+ and 12 ②f7 mate.

9 ③xg7! ②xg7 10 ③g1 ②fh5 11 ③g6 ♕d6 12 ③xd6 ③xd6 13 ②g6+ ③h7 14 ③xd6 Black resigns

Attack on the queenside

The targets of an attack on the queenside will primarily be weak pawns, but the aim of such an offensive may also be the invasion of the heavy pieces, usually the rooks, into the enemy position. Sometimes this invasion is transformed into an attack on the king, sheltering on the other side of the board.

We will begin with a classic example.

Rubinstein–Salwe
Lodz 1908

Black has a weak pawn at c6. It is instructive to follow how consistently the commander of the white pieces mounts on attack against it.

1 ②c5 ③fe8 2 ③f2!

Preparing to switch the rook across to the queenside.

2...②d7 3 ③xe7 ③xe7 4 ♕d4!

White maintains control over the c5 square.

4...♖ee8 5 ♗f1 ♖ec8 6 e3 ♕b7 7 ♘c5 ♘xc5 8 ♖xc5 ♖c7 9 ♖fc2 ♕b6 10 b4!

Now the black pawns are completely paralysed.

10...a6 11 ♖a5

White avoids the trap 11 ♖xd5?! cxd5! 12 ♕xb6 ♖xc2 with counterplay.

11...♖b8 12 a3 ♖a7

It is no longer possible to avoid the loss of a pawn.

13 ♖xc6 ♕xc6 14 ♕xa7 ♖a8 15 ♕c5 ♕b7 16 ♔f2 h5 17 ♗e2 g6 18 ♕d6 ♕c8 19 ♖c5

After winning a pawn, White does not hurry. The main thing is not to allow any counterplay on the part of the opponent.

19...♕b7 20 h4 a5

A desperate attempt to open up the position.

21 ♖c7 ♕b8 22 b5 a4 23 b6 ♖a5 24 b7

Black resigns. 25 ♖c8+ is threatened, and 24...♔g7 is met by 25 ♖xf7+.

With certain pawn structures, an offensive on the queenside has the aim of creating weaknesses in the opponent's pawns, and then attacking them. A typical example of such a storm is the so-called minority attack, when one, or more usually two pawns advance against the opponent's pawn chain.

In the following example White began a minority attack.

Averbakh–Ravinsky
Moscow 1950

1 b4 a6 2 a4 ♘g4 3 ♗xe7 ♕xe7 4 ♘xg4 ♗xg4 5 b5 axb5 6 axb5 ♕g5 7 ♔h1 ♖ad8 8 bxc6 bxc6

The two sides have consistently carried out their respective plans – White has opened lines on the queenside and has created a weak pawn in the opponent's position at c6, while Black has switched his queen to the kingside and is threatening the rook manoeuvre ...♖d6-h6. White must play very carefully, to avoid coming under a crushing attack.

9 ♘e2 ♖d6 10 ♖b6 ♖h6

Black gives up a pawn, to gain time for his attack. However, 10...♗d7 was correct, retaining the pawn for the moment, to which White was intending to reply 11 ♘g3, and if 11...♖h6 12 ♗f5!, combining attack with defence. After 12...♕h4 he has the move 13 h3 in reserve.

11 ℤxc6 ♘g6

Black has two threats – 11...♕h4, with an attack on h2, and 11...♘h4, threatening the g2 pawn.

12 ♘g1! ♘h4

12...♕h4 could have been answered by 13 h3.

Now on 13 ℤxh6 Black was planning the spectacular reply 13...♗h3! 14 ♗xh7+ ♚f8 15 ♕c5+ ℤe7. White has only one defence, but a perfectly adequate one.

13 f4! ℤxc6

Black is rattled and loses without a fight. After 13...♕h5 14 ℤxh6 ♕xh6 White would still have faced the problem of how to realise his extra pawn.

14 ♗xh7+! ♚f8 15 fxg5 ℤxc2 16 ♗xc2 ♗h5

17 ℤf4 was threatened.

17 ♗b3, and White won.

Kotov–Ragozin
Moscow 1949

White's heavy pieces are concentrated on the c-file, but for the moment the c6 pawn is adequately defended, and on 1 b5 Black appears to have the reply 1...c5.

Yet Kotov nevertheless played **1 b5!**

It turns out that 1...c5 can be met by 2 dxc5! ♕xe5 3 cxb6 ℤxc3 4 bxa7 ℤxc2 5 ℤxc2, when the d4 pawn promotes to a queen at a8! Ragozin saw this combination, and played differently.

1...ℤac7 2 bxc6 ♚g7

2...♘xc6 is met by 3 ♗b5.

3 ♕b1! ♘xc6 4 ♕xb6 ℤb8 5 ♕xb8! ♘xb8 6 ℤxc7 ♕xa3 7 ♗xg6!

The fire is immediately switched to the kingside.

7...♘c6 8 ℤ1xc6! ♗xc6 9 ℤxf7+ ♚h6

Or 9...♚h8 10 ♗h7 with the threat of 10 ♘g6 mate.

10 f4! ♕xe3+ 11 ♚h2 ♕xe5 12 fxe5, and Black resigned.

Petrosian–Bronstein
Moscow 1967

Black's kingside is weakened, but cannot easily be attacked. White, on the other hand, has a queenside pawn majority and the obvious plan of b2-b4-b5. Black, for his part, is threatening a pawn offensive in the centre with ...f7-f6 and ...e6-e5.

1 b4 ♗g7 2 ♖b1!

Accurately played! White needs to open the b-file as soon as possible, to invade with his rook at b6.

2...f6

Black is in too much of a hurry. He should have played 2...♕c7, combining attack with defence.

3 ♘d3 ♗f7 4 b5 ♕c7 5 bxa6 bxa6

5...♖xa6 6 ♘b5 and 7 ♘d6 is unpleasant for Black.

6 ♖b6 e5

Black is consistent, although this attempt to initiate play in the centre meets with a tactical refutation. However, White's plan would also have born fruit after 6...♖fe8 7 ♕a4 e5 8 ♖xa6.

7 dxe5 fxe5 8 ♘xe5! ♕xc5

If 8...♗xe5 9 ♘xd5 ♕xc5 (9...♗xd5 10 ♕xd5+) 10 ♖xe5, with the threat of 11 ♘f6+.

9 ♖c6 ♕a7

The toughest defence was 9...♕a5 10 ♘xf7 ♖xf7, and if 11 ♕xd5 ♕xd5 (not 11...♗xc3 12 ♖g6+) 12 ♘xd5 ♗d4, when White still faces the problem of realising his extra pawn.

10 ♘g4!

The rook, together with the knight, actively join the attack on the kingside.

10...♔h8

After 10...h5 the simplest is 11 ♘f6+, while if 10...♔h5 11 ♘xh6+ ♗xh6 12 ♕xh5 ♕xf2+ 13 ♔h2 ♕xe1 14 ♖xh6 with a decisive attack.

11 ♘xh6 ♗e8 12 ♖xe8! ♕xf2+ 13 ♔h2 ♖axe8 14 ♕h5 ♕e1 15 ♘f5+ ♔g8 16 ♘xg7 ♖f1 17 ♕xe8+ Black resigns

Index of Players
and Analysts

Adams 91
Ahues 30
Alatortsev 37
Alekhine 22, 44, 67, 79, 101, 104
Alster 50
Andersson 23
Antoshin 49
Aronin 31
Averbakh 22, 27, 28, 29, 47, 52, 74, 75, 94, 96, 98, 99, 101, 106, 107, 108

Balashov 39
Baranov 8
Barcza 60
Bardeleben 88
Bauer 93
Betak 50
Betatski 65
Biyiasis 39
Blackburne 87
Bogoljubow 35, 50
Boleslavsky 46
Bonch-Osmolovsky 8
Botvinnik 75, 76, 102
Boudi-Bueno 22
Bronstein 109
Bukhman 83

Capablanca 50
Chekhover 18, 19, 37, 49, 82, 84

Chigorin 38
Chudinovskikh 58
Colle 24, 101
Csom 64
Cvetkovic 23

Engels 40
Estrin 96
Euwe 34, 44
Evans 80

Fischer 43, 63, 105
Flohr 46, 83, 97
Fridstein 31, 99
Fuchs 101
Furman 33
Fuster 96

Gauffin 29
Geller 81
Georgadze 25
Gilbert 20
Gligoric 63
Gogolev 67
Goldberg 98
Greco 85

Hairabedian 65
Hoch 34
Hofman 59
Horberg 47

Isakov 32
Ivanov 59

Janowski 38

Kaminer 43
Kan 37, 46
Karpov 24, 64
Kasper 51
Keres 39
Kling 42
Klyatskin 39
Konstantinopolsky 37
Kopayev 74
Korchmar 68
Kotov 100, 109
Krogius 29
Kubbel 23
Kuindzhi 25
Kupper 48
Kurpun 30

Larsen 47, 77
Lasker, Em. 33, 48, 79, 93
Legall de Kermeur 20
Levenfish 46, 51
Lilienthal 83
Lyubensky 49

Maciewski 27
Magogonov 19
Manov 65
Marco 21
Maroczy 35, 40
Marshall 104
Matanovic 47

Matulovic 23
Mees 33
Menchik 75
Miles 59

Nedobora 60
Nikitin 32
Nimzowitsch 22
N.N. 24
Novoltenov 76

Olafsson 48
Ormos 65
Osloukhov 60

Parr 74
Perelman 86
Petrosian, A. 59
Petrosian, T. 104, 106, 109
Pillsbury 24
Polugayevsky 78
Polyak 68

Rabinovich 49
Radulov 73
Ragozin 109
Ravinsky 108
Reshevsky 44, 80

Richter 51
Romanovsky 66
Rotlewi 90
Rovner 76
Rubinstein 90, 107
Rudolph 85
Ryumin 51, 80

Sackmann 30
St Brie 20
Salwe 107
Sarvarov 107
Schmid 59
Sederborg 73
Shocron 43
Simagin 36, 97
Simkhovich 82
Sliwa 39
Smyslov 29, 33, 79
Solovyev 75
Soultanbiev 24
Spassky 77, 104, 105
Steinitz 88
Stepanov 76
Stolyar 52
Szepanek 49

Taimanov 29, 81
Tal 96

Tarjan 24
Tarnowski 60
Thomas 34
Tischler 32
Tolush 49
Torre, E. 23
Torre, K. 33, 91

Uhlmann 28, 59
Unzicker 100

Varshavsky 67
Vasyukov 79
Verlinsky 44, 80
von Popiel 21

Weltmander 78
Wheatcroft 74
White 30

Yates 67
Yudovich 39
Yurev 32

Zagoryansky 36, 102
Zhuravlev 58
Zita 29, 94
Zukertort 87
Zurakhov 83